He ain't he

By Dan Mely

CONTENTS

1	The Early Years	Page 6
2	It came from nowhere	Page 34
3	Dad got religion	Page 55
4	Bettws the top of the world	Page 69
5	Growing up rather quick	Page 88
6	Sign of the times	Page 99
7	The latter years	Page 118
8	The Family downfall	Page 136
9	life begins in his 40's plus	Page 145
	Butterfly	Page 166

FORWARD

This is a true story about my brother who I believe had a torrid life and was so misunderstood in a way that today would not be tolerated and was a heart-breaking existence which can now be explained in my mind. Dennis was mentally retarded but had a heart of gold but had no idea of how to express himself, he was unable to speak properly and this made his life hell inside his mind and I was a translator for him most of his life and because no one could understand him this made him nervous and frustrated, he lost his temper but was never violent to other people, he would just bite his fist and get into a rage until he was sometimes crying. In the beginning everyone thought Dennis was badly brain damaged but in my 50's I really believe he was as normal as you and I, I think he could learn to read and write but it was in his 40's he needed to be taught as his mind and brain worked about 25 years behind anyone else, he had normal feelings, he knew the difference between women and men had a sexual urge, and importantly he knew exactly what he wanted in life but was treated by his elders as if he was of no use to anyone and he let them believe that cleverly just to have peace and quiet. My story really starts during the second world war. Well mum was doing her bit for god and country by making bombs in the arsenal in Bridgend in South Wales for the war effort and dad was working for Baden Powell for the war effort as a minor in the coal mine in the Ogmore valley and as a member of the home guard, I can imagine the worry and fear they must of felt during this awesome time and did not realise the damage my mum's health would have after the war and for the rest of her life just by making these bombs that would kill millions of people in a far off country which I think she had serious misgivings about. The arsenal was not a place you would be able to work in these days with health and safety, today it would have been shut down, no masks or safety clothes to keep out the chemicals that would one day kill her. My father was a bit of a street fighter with his bare fists and was a man who would not take any nonsense from anyone, he had a bad temper and I sometimes wonder how my mum met him as she was so quiet. I remember him telling us about a man who tried to get off with mum and he was a boxer not just any boxer but a real good boxer and my dad wanted to sort this man out and so it was decided as most things like this was solved in those days that it would be in the Ogmore Vale town hall in the boxing ring as gentlemen, dad agreed and could not wait for this to happen thinking this would be a walkover. This night arrived and many came to see the fight, dad this time however had to wear boxing gloves and there they were standing either side of the referee and told they had to fight to the rules. So on they went dad for the first round took a bashing and never laid a glove on the boxer the same in the second round and dads face was covered in blood and eyes blackened and in a mess, well the third round and the same happened dad had not laid a glove on the other man and they sat down at the end of the round dads corner man wiping all the blood of his face, dad spitting blood in a bucket and face swollen and the next thing the other man threw the towel in the ring as he could not go on he was exhausted, well dad was not having any of this and shouted "You can't do this I haven't laid a bloody glove on you yet come on my turn now let's get on with it." but the man was done for although he had not got a scratch on him or any swelling at all he was just out of breath and dad was going mad in his corner with many people holding him back from killing this man who he never seen again from that night.

It was 1947 and my oldest brother was born Melvyn, he was born a healthy baby and later he would suffer with his eyesight as from an early age he was profoundly blind in one eye, Mel however got used to his problem and got on with life and he turned out to be one of the most impressionable men and a funny and loving character with the heart of a lion, however in 1949 everything went wrong yes Dennis came into the world and right away there was problems he was very deformed so badly no one expected him to live he had no roof to his mouth a cleft pallet a deformed upper lip and was mentally retarded there was no hope for him was the opinion of the doctors but mum and dad was not having any of this. Dennis had the problem that if he had to feed he needed to swallow he could not do this as he had no roof to his mouth and it is a fact that if you have no roof to your mouth you cannot swallow and if you tried to eat you would choke to death, and In them days nothing could be done surgically for him and so they decided he would not live out the first year.

Back in mum's family home and a brilliant device was put into action that would save Dens life, my Nan mum and dad took it in turns to feed Dennis day and night constantly to keep him alive, how? Well a simple way by using a rubber ink sucker out of an ink pen they just carefully kept his mouth open and dripped the milk straight down his throat with minute drops so as not to choke him this was a pain staking way to keep someone alive but it was the only way. Well Dennis thrived and grew in no time but it was a cruel world then as many people in whispers were saying it is wrong what they were doing to that little boy they should let nature take its course and let him die, this was only the beginning of these cutting whispers, my parents and us brothers would have to listen to in Dens lifetime it was so cruel what people would say not ever able to understand what mum and dad went through to keep him alive. Two brothers born and problems with both of them are the first signs of these chemicals from the arsenal days starting to affect my mother and family? Well in a few years Dennis grew up strong enough to be able to have some surgery to create a plastic roof to his mouth and this gave him a lot of hope for the future, however his mouth was still deformed enough to affect his speech he was difficult to understand when he spoke and that was not the only thing wrong he was incontinent and did nothing to try and control it he thought it was ok to go to the toilet in your pants and so he did, he had no understanding between right and wrong this would prove to be a big problem in future years.

April 3rd 1954 and lo and behold I was born into the world and I was born perfect no problems however I was one of twins and my sister was born dead why? Well the doctors said she was starved and all the nourishment went to me, or had the arsenal struck again was this to do with the chemicals in my mother's body doing this I wonder. Well they named me Daniel and I just ate and ate and got bigger until I started recognising things happening around me and my childhood began in a new village that was being constructed on top of a mountain in the middle of nowhere this place was called Bettws and this is where I remember my life beginning, a village built out of concrete slabs houses pre-stressed with steel, a way of building houses very quickly because of the shortages of housing due to the war and believe me they went up quick, they could do 2 houses in 6 days I think there were roughly around a thousand two hundred of them in total and just 2 little shops and a café come chip shop. I remember myself and Dennis running over tumps of earth like lots of little mountains with no roads this was fun for us as we were one of the first families there and not many people to give us any problems and my problems had not started because of this we could get covered in muck and no one to say anything to us except mum she would clean us up before dad got home, he was now working in the local power station which could be seen below our village and he had a huge motorbike a Panther with a side car that he would ride back and forth to work. These early days for me and Dennis were fantastic dad had rabbits he would breed for showing and for meat and some chickens for eggs and meat vegetables growing in all gardens including the front garden no lawns if you could not eat it dad wouldn't grow it, he was still living in the war days I am sure.

It was not long before houses took shape and many streets were born and Bettws took shape and along with it came our new neighbours and they were from all around wales all brought together in this big melting pot around about three and a half thousands of them, then the street lights came on and life was about to take a huge amount of getting used to, people would tell their children to stay away from Dennis as he was mad and if he comes near them come in and tell their parents, lots of whispering and looks that could kill these poor ignorant people were deluded what did they think he was going to do to them, but I shall start my story at the beginning.

CHAPTER 1

THE EARLY YEARS

Den started school as any other child did, he was expected to learn the same way and the school was a few doors away from my grandmothers, that was my father's mother and no one messed with her, she was a no-nonsense person. Well here goes, the first day Dennis sitting in his new classroom and he is sitting with all strangers, he knows no one at all. Teacher looking at Dennis and says to him "what is your name boy? "Den looks at him in wonder and smiles with his crooked smile but says nothing. The teacher in a sterner voice said. "You boy, I am talking to you, don't look at me stupid answer me." Den looks and smiles and points to himself and says "Dennis Duckfield." But due to Dens speech impediment he does not understand him, thinking he does not understand him and thinking he was being funny he proceeds to snarl at Dennis. "Speak properly, I did not understand that at all, come here and stand in front of the class and we shall see if we can't sort this out." Den just sits there and smiles and scratches his ear then the teacher lurched forward and grabs Den by the arm and pulls him hard up and in front of the class and says to him. "Now stop that silly grin and tell us your name clear and precise if you please." Den was now upset and serious and starts biting his thumb and looking frightened and he says "Dennis Duckfield listen I don't shout." The teacher laughs and lets Den's arm go and says. "I didn't understand any of that, anyone know this person? "A little lad sticks up his hand and the teacher says. "Yes lad. "Young lad speaks up. "He is Dennis Duckfield sir, he can't speak properly and he is mad my mother says." Teacher then says. "Yes, thank you lad I am not concerned what your mother thinks. "He turns to Den and says. "So, your Dennis Duckfield you have a brother in this school named Melvyn he is a pretty clever lad unlike you, you can't even pronounce your name properly, we will sort that out pretty quickly I'm sure. Sit down and pay attention." Den looking sheepish sits down and decides in his mind he is not going to like it there.

It was morning play time and Dennis decides its time to go home and legs it up the road, he runs into his grandmother and she could see he had been upset and asks. "What's the matter boy? What's happened?" She could feel he was shaking and Den says. "That man hurt me in the school, he pulled my arm off, go and kill him Nan. "Nan "I thought you would have trouble with that teacher he is a bloody idiot, well I'll give him something to think about now." She rolls up her cardigan sleeves and grabs Dennis's hand and she takes him back to the school as soon as playtime was over. She storms into the classroom with Den and goes right up to the teacher and says. "What the hell have you been doing to my grandson?" Teacher replies "Oh there he is, he is not good at discipline, is he? I was just coming to look for him do you know he is a little stupid? It took him twenty minutes to understand and tell me what his name was this morning." Nan stared at the teacher and says. "And so, you roughed him up so as to frighten him into telling you? Aren't you brave? Well let me tell you something." She grabs him by his jacket collar and his tie and pushed up the tie tight to his throat and says "If ever I hear you have laid a finger on him again or give him any sort of bad treatment, I shall be back here to sort you out and I do not make idle threats, I mean it." The teacher stutters and replies. "I am trying to do my job and I must discipline the children and that's final Mrs Duckfield." Nan turned and took Dennis and sat him in his seat, turned around looked at the teacher and said "Don't let me come back here again for the same reason, my other grandson will keep me informed, good day Mr Lewis." Nan stormed out of the classroom but it was on another day Dennis was in the playground where he had most of his trouble, kids continues to make fun of him and Melvyn had a hard time stopping it and then Dennis started to fight back with Mel until most of the kids left him alone except on odd occasion. Then the tables would turn and complaint after complaint would get back to mum, dad and my grandmother. He was becoming unmanageable in school and he was just not learning and things went from bad to worse.

Dennis was playing one day and he said to another lad. "Who is that little girl who is with you in the mornings? I like her." Another lad says to him "She is my twin sister look she is over there." Den turns around and looks and says. "Let's go and play with her. "Den and friend go over and the three play together Hailey and her friends start poking fun at Dennis and he gets upset. They were laughing at the fact he had dirtied in his pants and they were holding their noses and laughing out loud, Den starts biting his fist and in a tearful voice says. "I hate you to, I will tell the teacher and your brother if you don't leave me alone. "Den was red in the face by now and furious and a crowd gathered around. Then a teacher came up to see what all the noise was all about. Teacher says "Oh my god what a smell, is that you Duckfield? Look at the mess on you, I must get your mother to come and sort this out, your dirty little bugger that's naughty, don't come near me stand over there until I can get your parents to sort this out. "Den goes off to stand in the corner and mutters consistently to himself in anger. After a while his mum comes around to see Dennis standing there without a care in the world and the headmaster walking with her telling her off about the situation. "You must understand we cannot have this sort of thing in this school, we must sort this boy out he is totally unruly and is still not out of nappies yet, why? You or his father must discipline him and stop him doing this or he will be expelled from this school, do you understand?" Mum replies with sad voice "Yes I will get this sorted out with my husband. "Headmaster then says "I hope so I really do."

Mum walks up to Dennis and says. "What am I going to do with you Den this can't go on you must try Dennis, you must." Dennis turns and says with a loving smile "I got a girlfriend her name is, I forgot." Mum is almost in tears as kids are staring out of the window and giggling and the mess is running down Dens leg and they both look very sorryful standing there.

They walk back up to the grandmother's house and straight in the bath with him. He is sitting in the bath and mum says. "What is to become of you I wonder? You are not any good at anything and we love you but you are turning our lives upside down. "Nan speaks up "What have the doctors said the last time you seen them? "Mum moving shiftily replies "I don't understand what they are on about, they say he has a mental problem and want me to put him in Hensel castle for tests and if he has a mental problem, I can leave him there but surely, he can eventually learn? Do you think he is mad?" Nan "Well who knows what is going on in his little head, I'm damned if I know but there is something seriously wrong." Mam "I know. "Mum starts crying with her hands over her face, and then Den sees mum crying and says. "Don't cry mum I will be good, it was them not me, I don't want to go to school and look at me dancing mum." Mum looks up with tears in her eyes and replies "But you must go to school or I will end up in jail, what am I going to do? "Mum walks out of the room in tears and Nan bows her head as Den carries on playing as if nothing had happened. Dennis did not realise that Hensel Castle was for the people with dangerous levels of mental problems including padded cells and most of them in there were just left there for life like caged animals and forgotten about.

In the evening and mum and dad was sitting and talking about what had happened. Dad "So the head teacher was not happy then? I will have to get some time to go and see the school and see what I can sort out, do they want us to take him out of the school or what?" Mum says "I don't know what the hell they want us to do, I am at my wits end he has not got any better at all, the problem seem to be getting worse and yet Dennis doesn't seem troubled with it, it seems as if he is oblivious to it all and if we take him out of there where is he going to go? There is nowhere else to put him unless we move or we put him away." Dad says "What do you mean? In a mental hospital or that asylum Hensel castle you mean? Over my dead body." Mum replies "It's allright for you, you haven't got to sort this out every day, people looking at you and murmuring and staring as if we have a lunatic on our hands. I am not from this area and am shunned by the neighbours because of him, it's hopeless I can't take anymore." She starts crying again, dad looks at her and bows his head and says "I shall sort this out this week I promise, we can't put him in an asylum." Mum wiping tears away says "I know I was just sounding off, I love him so much but people here are not giving him a chance at all, please sort this out for him if not for me and poor little Mel is having a hell of a life because he is his brother and he is continuously fighting over Dennis and he is very young to do this."
Dad puts his arms around her and she gives a little smile. Dad says "There that's better, I will change shifts with someone so as to get in there in the next few days and I shall sort them out and I will try and reason with them, I am sure they will see reason and try to help, so dry your eyes if there was work somewhere else I would go there and we could try some where new to try and fix things but I can't lose this job or we just as well give up. It's the only work around as you know." Mum smiles and says "I know I wish I could do something to help, its hard but we will survive, don't worry I am

just being silly and as you are having some time off you can go and see the doctor about your eyes and find out what is happening there."

Dennis was sitting in the garden playing with his dog Queenie a black Labrador and giggling as they play. Dad goes and talks to him "Dennis, hello what are you doing to that dog?" Den replies with a loving smile "I love her she is funny, she licked me again, did you see her? She loves me, doesn't she?" Dad smiles and says lovingly "Yes she does, do you love mammy?" Den "Yes." Dad "Do you love me and Melvyn?" Den smiles and says "Yes." Dad "So what have you been doing in school to upset your teacher? I hope you did not do anything in your pants again, did you?" "No, I can't remember." Dad with serious look on his face "I think you did and you told me you won't do that again; you will have to say sorry to the teacher tomorrow ok?" Den "I am not going there anymore I hate it; I don't need school nanny says I am not going there again." Dad "No she didn't nan would not say that; I think your telling fibs and you are going back to school tomorrow if I got to drag you there myself and you will say sorry to the teacher ok?" Den starts crying and refuses to answer and lays flat on his tummy and covers his head and dad says to him "Your mum will tell me if you don't do as your told and I will smack you if you don't listen and I will be talking to your nan and she will give you a row for telling lies. So up to bed mister, go on, I mean it." Den gets up and howling, he runs up to bed.

Well it was 2 days later and dad went to the school and was in the headmaster's room and they were talking headmaster says to him "It's just a hopeless exercise, he is unmanageable he does not listen to a thing, he is incontinent, he is unruly, hyperactive, and lacks any intelligence at all. We are failing to get him educated." Dad replies "I can't see that, he is not like the other kids of his age so we must all take that into consideration, he must be educated and your supposed to be the professionals, this is ridiculous he is only 5 years of age he surely can learn if you put your minds to it?" Head teacher then says "Don't you think we have tried? He is impossible to teach it's hard to explain, he is so far behind the other pupils it's just not happening, he cannot learn it is hard to take in but he is incapable of learning and I am calling a meeting of the educational officer from the local council to see what can be done about this. It needs somebody who has loads of time with him alone and then I still think he is mentally retarded enough that he can't learn and I am sorry but that's how it is and nothing will change my opinion." Dad sits there and the blood in him was now boiling and he says "So what are we supposed to do with him? I can't teach him and my wife tries hard with him, what shall we do then? Give up and what take him up the woods somewhere and dump him."
Head teacher "I can't see any future for him other than if I can be honest is a lunatic asylum, put him there and get on with your lives he will be better off there with his own kind. I see absolutely no future for him." Dad sat there with hands clenched and says "If you had a childlike Dennis would you do the same?" Head master "It may sound cruel but I would." Dad

"Then you should not be here teaching children as you have no compassion, I am sure if he was yours you wouldn't do it so I will wait and see what the council say on the matter, good day sir." Dad stands up and storms out off up the road into nans house raging like a bull.

Sitting there was Nan and mum waiting for him to come in. He starts raving in a loud voice "He is a bloody maniac, he reckons Dens mentally retarded and he should be put in an asylum and we should then get on with our lives, who the hell he thinks he is?" Mum says "He said that? Your kidding we can't do that, oh god what are we going to do?" Nan chirps up "Oh he did, did he? Well we will see about that when I get my hands on him." Nan puts her cardigan on and rolls up her sleeves, dad turns around and stops her and says "Wait mum it's no good he is not going to listen and there is more, he has organised a council educational department meeting to see what they can do about Dennis and his future next week and we must abide with their decision by the looks of it." Nan sits back down and says "I don't believe it, that poor lad has no chance, they have decided by the looks of it so what are we going to do if they decide to expel him from school?" Mum says in a concerned voice "They can't do that I will never manage him on my own, I just can't there must be something we can do, I will end up in a mental hospital before long if this continues." Dad says "Just calm down Eileen no decision has been made yet, you never know the council will probably be on our side and tell them to pull their finger out stop blubbering and get on with their jobs and until then we must hope for the best." Mum says "I hope your right for Dens sake alone, that boy has not had any luck since he was conceived let alone the 5 years he has been alive." Nan says in reply "Yes Eileen your right it has been a battle for that boy all his life and with every year it is getting harder for him and I for one will do everything I can for him until the last breath in my body believe me."

It was the next day and Dennis went to school and I wonder if he really is that stupid as he seemed to finish his days by finally making their minds up for them. He went into the boy's cloakroom while they were all in lessons filled the plugholes up with toilet paper and turned all the taps on full and went into class and ended up flooding the school, he had all the teachers running around all that day it was so funny. I think he knew what he was doing all along it certainly sealed his fate, but he had a damn good thrashing by the headmaster before he left.

It was 2 weeks later and the day started just like any other, Dennis and Melvyn were in school and mum was with the dog queenie sitting in the house and a knock on the door came. She went and answered it; it was the postman. Mum speaks to the postman "Something for me?" Postman "Yes Mrs Duckfield a registered letter it looks important and I need your signature." Mum signs the piece of paper and he hands her the letter "There you are Mrs Duckfield see you again." Mum replies "Yes thanks." She walks back into the house and stares at the letter then she opens it and reads it. After a while she drops her hands with the letter and starts crying out loud, the dog comes over to her and looks puzzled at her but the tears were rolling down her face, mum cries "Why? Why? I can't take anymore I really can't, I don't see any point in going on, the world and every one in it hates this family, oh well girl even though you're a dog I think you have more compassion than any human." It seems that the news was not good for Dennis after all.

It was some time later and mum, dad and Nan were sitting there Dennis and Melvyn were out in the back yard playing with the dog. Nan asks "So what did it actually say in the letter?" Dad in stern voice says "It says and I quote, after considerable consultation and thought in this matter we all find that Dennis is incapable of learning without doubt and will never be able to do so and will never be able to contribute anything to his future and so it is with regret we feel that he would be a disreputable influence on other pupils and without further notice be excluded from the school, notice to take effect immediately etc. etc. no reply required just don't send him to school again and the council are coming around at our convenience to discuss what is to become of your son." Nan gives her opinion "It's ridiculous they can't do that, it's not right, there must be something we can do about it surely?" Mum "Not a thing it looks like I am going to serve life with Dennis around my ass for the rest of our lives and all the people still smirking behind our backs especially the neighbours, I hate it here and it was a lovely place for us until Den was born, since then it has been hell. It goes to show how cruel they can be. I can't see any life for us here, anymore can you?" Nan says tearfully "It may seem bad now but it can only get better, it will seem like nothing in a few years, but what is going to happen now?" Dad "Well life goes on, we can't change things we are caught between a rock and a hard place its difficult enough to survive on the money we have coming in but like you said it can only get better, look at them 2 playing with that dog out there? If only they knew the trouble, we are in." The 2 boys were having a great time in the garden running around with the dog then nan chirps up "Yes we can only hope this country improves after the last war, it seems it was us who lost with all the poverty here." Mum speaks "I think we had better get the kids in before they start down stairs again because I will swing for them if they start again tonight." Nan says "Oh stuff them I will sort them out if they start again don't worry, they are a pair of bloody idiots, they can't stop them grandchildren of mine enjoying life you leave them to me." Mum "No you don't understand they make my life a misery now and most of the time they won't talk to me; I wish they had kids the miserable cows so get them kids in for bed Ray." Dad gets them in.

Well it was a few weeks later and the council had made a time to meet with mum and dad, they looked very official sitting there and the older man started to speak "As you can see from our letter we took a lot of time over our decision about Dennis and we are sorry we had to come to that decision, however we have come with a couple of suggestions we would like to put to you." Dad butts in "Why are you so sure that Dennis can't learn?

What do you base that on? Are you experts?" The older man replies "Yes, I consider we have the qualifications to make this decision on the basis he has not been able to pick up any skills in reading writing or personal skills such as toileting and interaction with other children, don't you agree? Have you any proof he has?" Dad looks sheepish and says "Well he has good points also, he is not a bad lad, and what are we supposed to do with him? We are struggling as it is? "Older man says "So you agree with our findings?" Dad "Not entirely, I don't I think in time he will start to learn." Older man "By that time he would be about 7 years behind if he ever learns anything at all and in our opinion, he will never be capable of learning anything, he is retarded and that is it so we are going to suggest 2 things for Dennis's future and hope we get it right for everyone concerned. We have spoken to your doctor and we agree he should be sent to Hensel castle mental hospital for assessment for a month to six weeks and secondly after that assessment if he is as bad as we think he is he should if found of a severe mental state he remains there for the rest of his life if he is deemed to be of a danger to the public, can I have your reaction to this matter?" Immediately mum starts crying and Dad bows his head in despair, dad then speaks up as if he is defeated "Are you serious? Is that your answer to our problems? Just to chuck him into an asylum and leave him there and never think about him again as if he never existed, you must be off your head." Older man "What other choice do you have? You cannot educate him and so he is of no use to anyone if he is proved to be unsafe what choice do you have? "Dad with a face like thunder says "Do we have any choice as his parents? Or have you already decided? because if you cannot prove without a shadow of a doubt, he is unsafe to the public I will be bringing him home after these assessments and this is something my wife and I assure you. So, don't threaten me about my son." By this time mum was breaking her heart and dad was near to tears and the older man replies "Ok I agree, we shall decide again after the assessment. We shall arrange for him to go to Hensel castle in a few days." Dad snaps at the man "A few days, what is the hurry? Who the hell do you think you are? If I came into your house and said to you, I am taking your son or daughter away in a few days and you are not going to see him for six weeks what would you say to me? So, you give it a few weeks before you arrange this for me and the wife to get our heads around this ok?" Older man "Well it's my decision but I shall bow down to your request, 2 weeks it is then, I am sorry but I am just doing my job, I will say good day to you then." The both men leave and leave mum and dad sitting there crying and upset in each other's arms. Next in runs Den with queenie in tow, he speaks "Hello." Mum and dad wipe the tears away from their cheeks and Den then says "Why are you crying? I'm not." Mum bends down and cuddles him and says "We are just a little sad today." He jumps up onto the couch and says "Don't cry mummy look I can still dance." With that mum pours a ray of sunshine over him with a huge smile.

Well things settled down a little and mum was spending most of the days in the house with Dennis with most of the time having no one to talk to and

Dennis was spending most of his time in the garden with the neighbours looking on with resentment for Den because he was just retarded which was something frowned upon in those days as if it was caused by the parents because of past sins so that's why he had been stricken down as a punishment for his parent or parents past sins. It was a good thing Den was like he was as he didn't care what they thought of him but their cruelty had not come to the full yet. Well the day come for Den to leave for a few weeks away from mum and dad and he was told he was going on a great adventure; little did he know what was about to face him and also mum and dad.

They arrive at Hensel Castle and they felt as if all eyes were on them, they had a tour of the place it was a very old set of buildings and looked very intrusive and frightening and very much like as it is called a castle or dungeon and everyone was so serious. As they went around, they could hear screaming and came across many locked doors but when they asked what was behind them, they were virtually ignored. it then came time for them to leave Dennis behind this would prove to be the hardest thing they had ever done and Den held onto their hands tightly and all of a sudden dad said to him holding back the tears "Well we have to leave now and your adventure will start now, you must be good and have fun ok?" Next thing mum had a tear in her eye and Den could sense things were not right and started screaming and crying, a nurse held Den by the hand and started to lead him off but he struggled free and run up to mum and wrapped himself around her leg, she grabbed him and cuddled him as he was crying Den then said "I'll come with you mum, I am coming with you I am not staying here without you, I am coming home to see Mel and queenie, we will go now." By this time mum was breaking her heart and said to him "I will be here I will look after you don't cry, don't cry." With that the nurse grabbed Dennis and pulled him away from mum and carried him screaming up the corridor and you could hear him crying "Don't leave me, don't leave me, I must come home with you for queenie, dad come and get me quick, quick I'm scared dad, dad mum, mum." By this time mum could hardly stand with all the grief and collapsed onto a chair and dad was barely able to speak holding back the tears for mum's sake then mum spoke "Ray I can't do this I really can't do this, I must take him back with us it is breaking my heart, it really is." She sobs even more, dad puts his arms around mum and comforts her and speaks "We must do this to have any sort of future for him because if we take him home they will only come and drag him out of the house and that will be worse for him and us, it is killing me as well, let's just get out of here before I start crying too, he knows we love him and he needs this assessment for us all to know what to expect for the future." Mum wipes her face with her handkerchief and looks at dad and says "Yes I know your right but it hurts so bad and it seems this is all out of our hands and we have nothing to say about it, it feels as if he belongs to someone else now and we have no say what happens to him and that breaks my heart." Dad says "Yes I know I feel the same way but don't worry he will be back with us soon I am sure of that." Mum who has now stopped crying says "I wonder if it would be better to just leave him here and let him have his own life because if this is how it is going to be for the rest of his life, I could not bare it and he cannot take this for the rest of his life. It might be the answer for his sake, maybe we are being selfish and should let him go to be with kids of his own kind, he needs to have a happy life, we might just be holding him back, and I just don't know what to think." She starts crying again. Dad raging "Eileen that will never happen I will come and drag him out of here if they try and keep my son, forget it, it will never happen, over my dead body."

Back at home again Mel comes in from school and says "Where is Dennis mum? "Dad snaps "Sorry son he is not coming home for a while. "Mel starts crying and said "Why? He is not stupid like everyone says he is, he is my brother, he can't stay there please go and get him back dad. "Nan butts in "Melvyn don't worry he will be back; he is only having some tests to see if we can help him more. "Mel still crying replies "Nan he can do lots of other things and he will be crying if we leave him up there, he needs Queenie or he will die. "Mum "Don't be silly Mel he can go without Queenie for a while, he will be ok, you can look after Queenie till, he comes home, again can't you? " Mel "Yes but I need him home to help me I can't do it by myself, he is my little brother and he should be with us, please go and get him dad." Dad snaps "Melvyn just shut up and get up to bed if you are going to keep on, we must do as the doctor says now just get to bed now, go on." Mel runs up the stairs and nan looked at dad nasty and said "Ray you are so stupid sometimes, that poor lad just wants his brother that's all, he is hurting too you know and he is only a child himself and he has more than you to put up with because of Dennis." Dad "You all talk as if Dennis is a monster, everyone having to put up with Dennis, people are always saying that as if he is a mad dog or something, I will bring up my sons as I please, mum stay out of it." Mum then says "That lad does know how much trouble he has brought this family no getting away with it, so let's not try and pretend he is not the problem, but it's not his fault is it?" Nan "I think we must wait and see how things go for this first time for Dennis then decide the future, I know it is hard leaving him up there but it's not forever is it?" Dad "It will be if they have their way though." Mum looking daggers at dad says "Don't say that it is not going to happen. "

Things are not good mum now finds she has time on her hands that she has never had since Dennis came into her life and she is out to the shops again one day she is in one of the shops and an older lady from the village comes up to her and speaks "Well my dear I shall not condemn you I think it is a brave thing you have done letting that child go into a mental asylum, he is better off the streets and we will all feel safer from now on because you just can't let someone like him grow up in today's society can you? I think that was the only good thing Mr Hitler was right about mental illness is safer sorted out for everyone's sake because there is not a cure is there?" Mum stood there with a shocked look on her face and started crying and ran off. Mum hardly went out again for some time. However, my Nan found out about this and soon put people right and the neighbours came out into their garden more now that Dennis was not there. Mum thought everyone thought that was its Dennis was gone for good, they had given him up. This was going to be a big shock to most of this community and mum and dad could not wait. Then one day dad came in from work and called mum to come and sit down and that he wanted to talk to her urgently. They both sit down and mum looks at my dad's face seeing there was something wrong says "Oh what's the matter? Its Dennis isn't it? What's happened to him? They will not keep him up there I don't care what they say the neighbours think he is not coming back, I wish we could get away from here." Dad butts in "Wait a minute just calm down, Its nothing to do with Dennis and stuff the neighbours this is about the doctor, I as you know went up to see him about my eyes and these headaches I am having and he spoke to me today and it looks as if we might have to move from here anyway as I have what he calls Stagmus in my eyes and it is caused by the pit." Mum looks in horror and says "Oh god I can't take anymore so you have to finish in the pit now? How are we going to manage with no money? I think I will have to sign myself in with Dennis as I am going out of my mind, are you going blind or what? What does this mean?" Dad speaks in a relaxed voice "I am not going blind and I will have to finish in the pits and wear glasses and find a job somewhere else and maybe I have found one in the new development of the Port Talbot steel works in a gang erecting tower etc. I am going down there tomorrow week for an interview and the money is better there." Mum says "God it's a long way to go for work but I suppose there is no work anywhere else, is there any places nearer to there we can rent?" Dad rubs his chin and says "No, not really I will have to travel until I can find a place nearer to there, I know that the village of Bettws is about to build a couple of hundred council houses there in the next 2 years, so I shall put our name down for one, fancy that?" Mum had a huge smile come over her face and says "Yes I will do anything to get out of this valley, anything, I just hope this will all work out, we could do with some luck."

Well the day came and they went up to get Dennis with a lot of wonder in their minds. Is Dennis going to be the same lad they left in there or could he be a changed person as mum and dad only had phone calls, they made to the officials there as they were not allowed to visit for fear of too much disruption for him? Well the time came and mum and dad sat in a waiting room, next in came Den and he just run straight at mum and never said nothing but just leapt into her arms and grabbed her really tightly. Mum spoke to him "Hello how's my little man then? Have you been a good boy?" There was no answer from him he just did not want to speak. Dad said to Den "Are you ready to come home? Queenie is waiting in the house to see you and Mel is missing you, he is waiting for his little brother to come home." There was no reaction from Dennis at all, he just held mum real tight and was not going to let go. Mum spoke to the matron "Right can we take him home now? We just want to get out of here." Matron looked surprised "Don't you want to know how he got on here?" Mum replies

"Mmm, not really, I just want to take him home." Matron "Well I'm sure someone will be in touch, I will say goodbye now, and goodbye Dennis we will see you soon." Mum says "What do you mean you will see him again? He will not be back here again." Matron chirps up "Oh I am sure the doctor said we will be having him back in a few weeks." Mum snaps at her "Over my dead body, I will not have him being your guinea pig, not on your Nelly so you can stick that in your pipe and smoke it." Dad looks concerned at my mum's outburst and speaks to matron "Please excuse my wife she has been under severe strain, you must understand this is not easy for either of us, we are off now if that's ok." Matron "Yes I understand, you must sign him out of here by the desk, goodbye." Dad says "Goodbye." They all leave the asylum and all the way home Dennis hardly says a word. They arrive home and he still hardly say much he just wants to have a drink and go to bed, so mum and dad tucks him in and he immediately goes off to sleep.

Back downstairs and Nan has arrived to see Den but she is too late and says "Where is he then?" Mum speaks "He has gone to bed and he has hardly said a word all the way home and even since he has come in through the door, he was happy to go to bed, I hope they haven't taken the boy out of him, what did they do to him? He is different. What have they done? Electric shock maybe tortures or something? If they have, I shall kill them." Dad speaks "Oh don't be silly they wouldn't do that, this is a civilized country and he is just a boy for goodness sake." Next nan puts her two Penarth in "You never know look what Hitler done to the Jews, gypsies etc., no one expected that but it happened." mum says "see, thank you mam I am not the only one it might have happened" dad "the pair of you are paranoid" nan "so what have they said?" mom "well the matron seems to think he is going back soon, but I don't think so I think this has been too much for him, I am not prepared to let them use him as a guinea pig and that is it" dad says the same nan "I agree I expect they will arrange to come and see you both again and give you the results" dad "something like that.

Well it was the next day and mum, dad and Mel were up and about but no sign of Dennis, and he lies in bed still until midday. Next in walks mum and Den had done it again he had dirtied the bed, mum sits him up and says "Oh dear Den you've done it again, well let's get you into the bath, aren't you speaking to me today?" Den looks up at mum and mumbles with a sad look on his face "Yes, where are we going today or shall I stay in bed?" Mum looks at him even tries to make him smile with some pathetic faces but no reaction, she says "We are not going anywhere babe, you can go out to play with Queenie if you like she is waiting for you. What do you think fancy that? And Mel will be home soon from school." Den murmurs again "Yeh." Mum takes him off for a bath and downstairs later Den spots dad in the garden and says to mum "Mum, mum, why is dad not in work? You said we were not going anywhere? He is not taking me back I am not going there again no, no, no." Dad runs in to see what all the fuss is about. Dad says in urgent voice "What's the matter Den why are you shouting at your mother?" Mum butts in "Hang on Ray he is upset, he thinks you are taking him back up to Hensel and that's why you have not gone to work." Den was sitting on the sofa sobbing. Dad speaks to him "Sh, Sh, Sh don't worry no one is taking you back there so don't be so daft." Mum says as Den stops crying "If I get my way you will never go there again so jump up and go out and give this bone to queenie and dad and me will make you your breakfast or dinner now, what do you think?" Den smiles and grabs the bone and says "If they come here again, we will shoot them and feed them to the dog that will teach them." He goes off to feed the dog his bone and mum and dad go into the kitchen. Dad speaks "I don't know what happened but they have frightened him pretty badly, I wonder what happened? Well we will have to sit down and talk this out before these idiots come back, we can't avoid it." Mum replies "Yes I know, I know let's just have a peaceful weekend for once, it's bad enough those idiot's downstairs are making my life hell wait until they see Den's back, they will start being funny again, why don't we just pack up and go a live in a tent in Bettws until those houses are finished." Dad replies "Wouldn't that be great I wish we could I would love that, I am not kidding I would just love that so would Den and Melvyn I'm sure but I don't think it will be so easy for you." Mum chirps up "Do you want to bet? I would live in a pig sty if I thought we would not have to come back here." Next thing Melvyn comes running in shouting "Dad next door have been shouting at Dennis and the dog, Den left the dog onto his garden and the dog pood in his garden, he told Den off." Mum says "Oh here we go I knew it, go and sort it out or I will swing for that bastard down there." Dad tries to cool mum down "Calm down Eileen don't let them get at you, I will sort it out now." Dad goes down the garden and out there was Den and the dog playing and the neighbour cleaning up the dog mess. Dad speaks to him "Allright George I heard my dog dirtied in your garden I'm sorry about that can I do something to help?" George snarls "Again it is happening all the time that lad of yours doesn't understand English, how many times have I got to tell him not to open the gate between us? He is so bloody stupid." Dad not very happy speaks back to him "I don't think there is any need for that he can't help it, he has some problems, we are trying to sort out." George still nasty stops dad in his tracks and says. "Some problems that's the understatement of the decade, he is simple and last week I thought he had been put away and my life was getting better but it is not to be, if I didn't have bad legs none of this would happen as I would show you how to discipline that kid." Now it is getting into a heated argument and dad says "I don't think so mate, my son would make ten of you, your lazy bastard. You have been swinging the lead since before the war because you are a shit house and afraid of his own shadow, so don't come it with me you're an arshole everyone says it." George retaliates "Well let me tell you now if I hadn't had that accident and damaged my nerves in my legs, I would come over there and make mincemeat out of you, just think yourself lucky." Dad laughs and says "You couldn't fight your way out of a paper bag a nutter, I am telling you if I ever hear your slagging anyone of my family off again, I will not speak I will just come in there and smack you right in the gob, got it? Now kids stay away from the gate." By this time George had gone in with a smirk on his face and dad goes up the path and was confronted by mum, she does not look pleased at all and speaks "Well done ray, you have just made things worse its allright for you, you will be in work and I will have all the flack for this, brilliant, brilliant." Dad had a smile on his face and says "Oh don't worry about it we will not be here for much longer and if he gives you any trouble I will go in there and sort him out ok?" Mum says "Oh there we are then, that's the answer to it all from now on I hope we do get out soon or my life will be hell."

Well life settled down for a while but mother could feel things were getting much worse and the neighbours being silent was like being sent to Coventry and nan was working in the day now and so mum and Dennis were alone for most of the day and dad by this time was now in the steel works in Margam in Port Talbot and it meant he was working later as he had to travel more than ever. They had put in for a house in Bettws and was waiting for that day to come and it could not come fast enough. Well the day came around again for the local government people to come back and try and make a decision about Dennis. This was going to be traumatic for the family never mind what they decide this was one day dad was not going to put up with any nonsense with any of them.

A knock on the door and dad, mum and Dennis were sitting there, Den had no idea this was about to happen and they were all on edge, dad gets up to answer the door. He speaks "Hello come in and sit down." They walked in and sat down, the older man says to mum "Hello Mrs Duckfield and hello Den how are you then?" Den just squirmed and cuddled up to mum, mum says "Say hello Den, oh he is very shy sometimes." Older man says "Oh don't worry he is alright, well I have had a report from the Hensel Castle people and I shall read it if you agree, is that allright?" Dad says "Well that's what you have come here for isn't it?" Older man "Yes, well here we go. This is from Mr Hughes one of the top consultants there. I have observed and got into some play schemes with Dennis and he is not a very bright lad and does not want to react with other people much and seems to be in a world of his own and does not seem to want to do what is right in a natural world like toileting and eating matters. He has no skills as regards putting the simplest objects together and what they represent does not care about it either. His interaction with other people takes time, he is so unsure of himself it is uncanny for a young child of his age not to react with other children. He does love to listen to any music and loves to dance a little, I was amazed how much he does love music and the television but wants to play with the television and record player and would want to do this at all times.

We observed him in all tests set him and his reaction to all of them was contempt and in my view, he is unable to learn, he is totally retarded in this matter and in my view, he has nothing he can contribute that is of any use to himself or others.

As regards how he reacts to other people and if I think he is a danger to himself or anyone he comes into contact with now and in the future. In my view Dennis is of reasonable character now as a child I think he will have the mind of a child even after his twenties, his mind is of a child 20 years younger than the age of his body and I think he will be reasonably harmless for the early years of his life and as regards further on in his life, who knows? I cannot predict how his brain will develop in the future and if I had to state categorically if he is going to be a danger to himself or his peers in the future I cannot tell at this stage and therefore I suggest a review with Dennis every 3 years at this facility and make judgment at these times and if in the meantime he becomes irritable towards others or his future changes so as to seem troubled or violent to others, he should be brought here and we will assess his future after a series of tests to determine his state of mind. "Well there you have it do you have anything to add?" Mum speaks up "This is all jargon to me, what does this mean I hope you don't think you are taking him away from us?" Younger man says "No it does not mean that at all, it just gives us guidelines to consider as regards the future and what to look out for with Dennis." Next thing dad chirps up "Who is this man to make these assumptions about my son? How does he know how Den will be in ten years? That's rubbish." Older man "Well we don't know how things are going to go, you, me, your wife, none of us so I suggest we work together to be sure nothing goes wrong, so he will be staying home with you and from time to time we will hope you agree to take him up to Hensel for a day or 2 for him to be assessed and that's it." Dad speaks to mum "Well what do you think mother?" Mum replies "What can I say? They have made their minds up, we can't do much about it can we? So, don't ask me." Older man speaks "No it's not like that at all, if we did nothing, we would be accused of that. We are just trying to help nothing else." Mum says "I bet you are, he is my child and I brought him into the world and I will decide his future." Older man says in a calm gentle voice. "Yes, I agree we will give you all the help we can like for instance if you need a holiday from Dennis just for a break for you and your husband and Melvyn to have a break Dennis will be welcome in Hensel castle for that period of time with no cost to yourselves." Next thing Den starts crying and buries his head in mums lap. Mum says "Listen to him he does not want to see that place as long as he lives, it frightens him so much." Younger man chirps up "That's because it is strange for him and children like him don't like change. If you and your husband stuck to your guns, he would get used to it and it would get easier every time and let's face it you would cope better after it as you would be rested and able to cope easier and it is not the law you don't have to take this offer up." Dad says "Ok we will think about it at least, is that it anything else?" Older man says "Well anything else we can help you with like ideas etc." Dad says "No I don't think so, oh wait you are on the council, can you help with accommodation like council houses?" Older man says "What do you mean? I don't understand." Dad continues "Well we have applied for a council house in Bettws when they are built but we need to get away from here as soon as possible. They have started clearing the sight I know as I pass there every day on my way to work in Port Talbot steel works." Older man says "You are travelling every day to Port Talbot to work from here and you have applied for a house in Bettws? Have they said you got one?" Dad says "Oh yes but there are a lot of houses going up, I may be the last one in but if I could get the family there as quickly as possible then it would take the pressure off us straight away and that would be a great help." Older man says "I don't see why not, I think this is an urgent matter and I shall go back now and go and see the people concerned. I am not promising you anything mind in case something goes wrong." Dad says "That will be great if you could." Mum with her head down says "I won't hold my breath it never goes right for us, never." Older man speaks up "Come on Mrs Duckfield chin up, I will do my best I assure you I think things are going to get better let's just wait and see." Dad shows them to the door and shakes hands with the older man and thanks him, he closes the door and comes back in with a big grin on his face and says to mum "Well that wasn't too bad was it? And hopefully we may move sooner than later. Come on let's go for a spin in the motorbike and sidecar, what about it love?" Mum looks up and says "Den do you want to go for a ride on the motorbike? And we can have a look at the sheep and have an ice cream on the top of the mountain" Den looks so excited and says "Oh yes let's take Mel and queenie with us, can I sit on the back, can I?" Dad in a happy voice says "No its too dangerous Den you are too small and I have no room in the sidecar for Queenie she is too fat and Mel is in school. You must sit in the back of the side car and mum in the front and you must look after your mum ok?" Den very happy by now says "Ok dad I will." Off they go and they went up over the Bwlch Mountain and had an ice cream on top of the mountain and Den was really enjoying himself and you could see the happiness on mum's face that's not been seen for a long time.

Well it was later that evening after the boys had gone to bed and mum and dad were talking down stairs and they were waiting for nan who promised to drop some fish and chips off to them on her way home. Mum speaks "That was a nice day after all. Dennis enjoyed himself on the motorbike, we must take Melvyn out though on the weekend, he felt a little left out I think and I have some news, I don't know if you think it is bad or good." Dad butts in "Your pregnant." Mum looks in amazement with her mouth open and says "You know? You know how? I only just realised." Dad says "I can always tell with you as your so skinny I can tell straight away, I have suspected for a few weeks now. Have you seen the doctor?" Mum replies "No I kept thinking I was but then sometimes I doubted it so I may be further gone than I suspect." Dad says "Mum said she was sure you were a couple of weeks ago but I didn't like to say anything until I heard it from your mouth." Mum says "And how do you feel about it? I thought you may be unhappy about it as if we haven't enough problems." Dad says "It's too late now we can't do anything about it now and I am ok with it, it might take your mind off things and Den is getting older and if we move to Bettws it will be great. There is so much land for them to run around in it is unbelievable, you wait till you see it. It will give us more time to get closer as a family." Mum says "Yes I suppose so and maybe I will have a girl for a change, someone to give me a hand around the place. I thought mum was looking at me strange sometimes, now I know why." Next Nan walks in with chips in paper. Dad dishes it out and Nan starts to get comfortable in dads chair. Dad teases her but he knows his place when Nan is there, they both laugh and mum speaks "Well you are going to be a granny again by the looks of it." Nan says "Yes I know, I knew you were I said it to Ray I have known for a while, shall I call in the Doctors tomorrow and ask him to call on my way to work?" Mum says "Yes you better, as I have no idea how far gone, I am, I was saying to ray I hope it's a girl, she could be helpful around the house hopefully in Bettws as we have more news too tell you, tell her Ray." Dad chirps up "Yes they called today and give us the results I have a copy for you to read and they are going to try and get us in Bettws as fast as they can build the house, so they say, so we might be gone soon." Nan says "Well, that's nice I think, so we are going to lose you? Well I can't say I will be happy for you to go, I will miss you all." Mum says "We will be back and forth don't worry as long as we don't have to stay in this valley much longer, you will still see a lot of us." Nan says "That's ok then, so long as I see the kids and my new grandchild as well, so things are looking up for you at last. Have you thought of telling them in the council about your new due arrival so as they can update the files and give you a larger house?" Dad says "Oh I never thought of that at all, I had better phone them in the morning. Anything else I have forgotten? "Nan "I don't think so, now let's see what they have to say about my grandson." Nan starts reading. Mum says to dad "I hope this is the start of our future, as I feel like screaming, I nearly did on top of the mountain today. I even had a smile off one of those ugly mountain sheep today up on that mountain. I feel it's our turn for some luck." Nan interrupts "The cheeky buggers, I hope they are still alive when Dennis is an adult and see just how lovely he is going to turn out, I don't think these people know what the hell they are talking about sometimes they guess if you ask me, I have more intelligence in my little finger than they have in their whole bodies, I'm sorry I have. So, is that it? Is Den going to have peace now?" Dad answers "They are going to assess him every 3 years as they think he might change and they are worried he may become violent, so they want to keep an eye on him just to be sure." Nan then says "Suppose they have to show they are doing something, I expect someone somewhere needs something to do." Mum says. "As long as they leave that boy alone and let him grow up a happy lad and not threaten him with Hensel castle I don't care. I think we might just as well put it in the back of our minds until it happens or it will drive me mad and I don't want to think about it. I am making a cup of tea anyone wants one?" They both say yes and mum goes out to the kitchen to make one. Nan turns to dad and says "She looks so tired, I hope she is ok. She has been through hell with all this nonsense, I think you should keep an eye on her, I don't think she can take much more." Dad says "Yes I know, I have been very worried about it all and this baby is coming at a hard time for her and I hope we don't have another Dennis, it would destroy us both. So, we need to give her as much support as we can." Nan agrees and says "I shall come over every morning to help and keep her mind off things until you move, don't worry it will be allright."

Well things went on with no problems for a few weeks and mum looked a much happier person and nan as promised called in every morning and dad was hardly about as he had a chance to get some overtime in the steel works which brought in some needed money. Then all of a sudden something happened and this was a very serious thing, it was a nice summer's day and mum went out to feed queenie and she was not about, this was funny as she was always around when it came to food, well mum went to the bottom of the garden and kept calling her and Dennis was also shouting to. Next in comes Nan, mum looking concerned says to Nan. "Well I can't find that dog anywhere I have been calling her for over an hour now, I hope she is ok." Nan replies "Yes she is out playing with the other dogs some where I expect, she is so loving she loves to play, she will be back when she is really hungry don't worry and how's my boy? He looks very happy with himself." Mum says "He made himself a cup of pop this morning and didn't spill a drop and he is so pleased with himself, he wants to do it every five minutes now." Nan smiling says "Well there you go then he is not so daft, is he? not anything like what they said, if you remember they said he was incapable of learning and he just made himself a drink that's a good start, he will be cooking dinner for everyone soon enough." Mum says "Oh I don't think so not even ray can do that, I won't hold my breath but yes, he is trying and proving them wrong." Next in comes Dennis looking so sad and says "Nan I can't see queenie anywhere, I want to play with her, come and see if you can see her." He tries to pull Nan out of the chair and Nan says "She will be back now don't worry, what's this I heard you made yourself a drink this morning, is that true?" Looking so important Den looked up at Nan with a crooked smile and says "Of course, I am a big boy now I can do drinks and smoke a fag like dads and drink beer like dad." Mum says "I don't think so young man I don't want to see you with any fags or beer in your hand, your too little." Nan says "No leave that to your dad and granddad he can put a couple a night away my god, he can't go a night unless he has had a pint and that bloody club he never misses going down there, I don't know how he does it he works that door just to get a couple of pints a night without fail." Mum says "I know he never misses does he? But there you are he never gets into any trouble and you always know where he is. He does no harm to anyone; I think the world of him such a considerate man and a proper valley man to boot." Nan speaks "I suppose so and he never misses work ever, I have a good one there, I can hear that boy out there crying I am going to see what's the matter with him, I will be back now." Nan trots down the garden and she sees Den crying and says "What's the matter young man? Why are you crying?" Den full of tears says "I want queenie and she is not here she always plays with me and I need to find her." Nan shouts up to mum "Eileen I am taking Dennis for a walk to find that bloody dog to get some peace and quiet." Mum shouts back "Ok don't be long."

Nan and Den walks down to the park and down the back lanes but no sign of Queenie anywhere. After an hour walking around, they give up and return to the house. They walk into the living room and Nan says "Well we have looked everywhere but no sign of her at all. Where the hell can she be?" Mum looking worried says "That's a mystery, I have never known her to disappear like this before, oh she will turn up soon I bet, you had better be off to work or the boss will be giving you the boot." Nan says "I don't think so he gets more than his money's worth out of me, he could never sack me or he would have to hire 2 people to do as much as me, but your right I will see you tonight, c'mon Den give me a kiss I will see you later and be good for your mummy." Den gives Nan a huge kiss and she says "Tata I will see you later." Mum says goodbye and off Nan goes

Well it was later when dad comes home from work and things were so tense due to queenie being missing. Dad comes in from work and says "Hello everything ok? Hi kids "Den and Mel run up to dad and give him a kiss Den says "Queenies run away, she has been gone all day." Dad says to them all "What do you mean queenie is missing? She is always about here somewhere, have anyone been out to look for her?" Mum says "Yes your mum has been all over the place looking for her this morning and not a sign of her anywhere." Dad says "Oh god, she is always around here somewhere she never goes off for long ever, I had better go and look for her I am worried now." Mel says "Can I come dad? I think she is hiding somewhere." Dad says "No son it's time for your bed and it will be dark soon so I had better hurry, give me a kiss goodnight and be good for your mum and go to bed like good boys ok?" Both boys agree and off they go. Dad says to mum "I am going out for a look around I will be as quick as I can." Mum says "Ok see you later." Dad goes off and he walks everywhere and no sign of Queenie, he is getting really worried by now, he asks everyone he meets but no one has seen her he remembers she liked to go up by the side of the school where the rabbits run wild and there was a stream there and she loved to paddle there and chase the rabbits so dad went up there and he turned around the end of the school wall and cocked his leg over the wall and got a huge shock, he could see a large black thing by the side of the stream, he run up to it and it was queenie she was still and lifeless. Dad bent down and realising she was dead he lifted her head up and with a tear in his eye said "What happened to your old girl? What happened? Why would anyone do anything like this to a loving dog like you, you never did anything to a soul, why? Why?" With a huge sigh and his eyes full of tears he picks up Queenie up in his arms and he takes her over under a large oak tree and lays her out and hurries home in a real temper. He gets to the door and mum sees he had been crying. She puts her hands over her mouth "She's dead, isn't she?" Dad in tears says "Yes she is, I must go and bury her in her favourite spot behind the school before it gets too dark and we will discuss it when I get back, I can't talk now." Choking back the tears he grabs a spade and leaves. Back at the school there is dad in front of queenies grave and holding her collar in his hand and saying "I will get the bastard who did this if it's the last thing I do."

Back at the house and mum and dad sitting on chairs. Mum sobbing and dad sitting with his head in his hands looking very sad. Next in walks Nan she speaks "Oh my goodness what's the matter? Please tell me why are you crying. "Dad speaks up in a quiet voice holding back the tears "Queenie is dead." Nan says with her hand over her mouth "Oh no, oh no not queenie oh what happened to her? That loving dog." Dad replies "I found her behind the school by the stream and she was dead and she had been dead for a long time and I don't know why but I will get the bastard who did this I swear I will." Nan asks "What do you mean was she shot? "Dad says "No she was poisoned with rat poison." Nan says "How do you know?" Dad replies "Her whole body was swollen and she went to the stream for the water because that's what rat poison does it makes you thirsty and once you have drunk the water the rat poison takes effect and it swells you up and kills you, she had no water left in her dish here so she made a mad dash for the stream and I know who done this and I will have him if it's the last thing I do." Nan says "Now cool down ray you must be rational about this and be sensible I think I know who you are on about, that jerk down stairs isn't it?" Mum speaks up "That's ridiculous even he can't be that cruel surely." Dad says "Who else could it be? He has had it in for us especially the dog and Dennis, no one else would do that but he will pay for it. "Mum concerned says "What are you going to do, he is a cripple and if you beat him up you would be finished and ridiculed right throughout the valleys. If he did it, he has got away with it, the best thing to do is ignore him but get the police involved isn't it?" Nan backs mum up "Eileen is right he will hide behind his handicap and the only one who will lose is you. "Dad shouts "And what about queenie she didn't deserve to die that dog was such a loving animal, she wouldn't hurt a fly and what am I going to say to those boys upstairs tomorrow? I don't know if I can keep my hands off him I really don't." Nan says in a calm voice "Ray I know you are hurting and I feel a lot of sadness for Queenie but I think there is nothing we can do just put it down to experience and let it go at that, he will get his up and commence later in life, I hope he does for queenies sake, have you buried her?" Dad says "Yes I buried her up by that huge oak tree behind the school where she used to chase the rabbits, she loved it there, but what am I going to say to the kids mum? What am I going to say?" Nan with a tear in her eyes says "This is a time that I can help if you will let me? I shall take them up to see where she is buried and tell them the way it is first thing tomorrow." Mum says "Ray I think your mum is the best one to explain to the boys, don't you?" Dad still looking sad says "Yes I think you are right because I don't know what to say to them as I am devastated, I can't wait to get out of this cruel valley, I never thought I would ever say this but that's how I feel." Nan says "Why don't you both try and get some sleep now, things may look better in the morning, I know it's easy to say that but life must go on and you are bigger than that idiot downstairs." Mum says "Are you ok ray? This has really got to you hasn't it? I know it has taken a big chunk out of me." Dad says "Yes it has, this is a cruel world and sometimes I wish I could get off it, I am going to bed if its ok with you I am up early in the morning, goodnight." Dad gets up and off to bed, mum and nan still sitting there and nan says "Well that takes the biscuit I never knew anyone could be so cruel, I have seen it all now that poor lovely dog I can't believe it, I just can't, the poor little darling." Nan starts to weep and mums says "When you leave later can you do me a favour? "Nan sniffing says "Yes of course what is it?" Mum says in a tearful voice "Can you pick up queenies dishes and take them home and bin them for me as I can't and it will upset ray and the kids so much." They both burst out crying for a minute or so and Nan pulled herself together and says "Of course and I will be up in the morning to take the boys up to the grave and explain it all to them." Mum wiping tears away says "Thank you mum we will have a hell of a time getting over this, be careful walking down the road I will see you in the morning." Nan replies "Goodnight Eileen, see you in the morning. "Mum says "Yes goodnight."

Outside you see Nan looking down at the dog dishes and she looks very sad, she bends down and picks them up and leaves for home.

It was the next morning around 10am and the boys were sitting on the sofa waiting for Nan and wondering why they were going for a walk with her and why they were dressed up smart. Next in walks Nan she says "Good morning my boys and how's nans boys today? Shall we go for a walk?" Melvyn says "Yes ok where are we going?" Nan says "We are going somewhere special today for Nan to tell you something secret." Den chirps up "What's that nana?" Nan replies "Well it wouldn't be a secret if I told you would it?" The boys grab Nan's hand and off they go down past nans house down the hill past the school and around the walls edge, around the corner over the fence and up to the big old oak tree, they both spot the mound of earth and wonder. Nan speaks to them "Do you know what that is?" Both boys nod no. Nan says "Well that is a special place for someone we all love, you see yesterday god told queenie he needs her up in heaven with him and she had to come straight away so she has gone up to heaven to be with god and your dad put her old body that she does not need anymore in the place she loved most." Melvyn starts crying and Den looked just as sad. Mel says "Queenie is dead, how? Why? When?" Next Den starts crying also so both of them was now sobbing and nan says "Oh dear I don't think queenie wants to upset you and make you cry, do you? She loved you both and it will upset her if she is watching now, so stop crying for queenie, she wanted to go to doggy heaven and she is happy and she asked me if you would both pick some flowers for her? What do you say? Shall we pick some flowers? She would like that." Both boys still sniffing say they want to pick flowers and off they go picking daisies and buttercups. They get a nice bunch each and lay them on the grave and with a little tear Den says "Will she be able to play with me anymore?" Nan looking sad says "I'm afraid not anymore, she is in heaven now and she wants you both to be happy but she will be looking down on you to keep you safe especially when you move soon, so just think she is around but you can't see her, she loved you both and wants you not to cry but be happy that you knew her, I tell you what shall we say a little prayer?" Both boys nod yes but seemed very upset. Nan says ok and she recites the Lord's Prayer to them over the grave and when they finished Nan says "Let's say goodbye to queenie one at a time, you first Den." Den says "Bye, bye little queenie bye." Next Mel says "So long girl I will miss you bye." Nan next "Goodbye old girl you were a wonderful animal and we will miss you very much, there will never be a dog like you again, goodbye." They all walk away looking very solemn and they stopped in nans house for an ice cream and some cakes. Mel still sobbing says to Nan "Is mummy having another baby nana? "Nan replies with a little smile. "Yes, she is so you will have another brother or sister to play with. "Mel did not look happy about the answer and moaned Nan says to him. "What's the matter Melvyn? Why are you not happy? " Melvyn "I hope the new baby will not be like Dennis, I will have to fight more of the kids around here if she is and I hate them as they make fun of Den and me all of the time, it's not fair." Nana looking solemn says "Oh Mel I know what you mean but it will not happen again, it's not Dennis's fault he is like he is so don't worry about it and do you have lots of trouble with other kids then?" Mel looking serious replies "Yes all of the time and it really hurts me and what they say about Dennis and I know he can't help it it's just not fair all of the time, it's every day nana. " Nan smiles and says "Well Dennis is very lucky to have a brother like you and your very special to all of us because you look after Dennis and things will get better as you get older Mel and with this new baby coming who knows it might be a girl and you will have a sister and she will sort them out I bet, so don't worry. "Mel says in serious voice "As long as she is not like Dennis and maybe she will be as nice as Queenie she was a loving dog. " he starts crying again and Dennis puts his arms around Mel to comfort him and says "Don't worry Mel I will look after you and the new baby, we can have lots of fun if you like, I will sort them boys out, I will bash them up for you." Nana and Mel smile at what he says and nana says "Yes that's right Den you will sort them out won't you? See Mel he loves you too; you will see things will get better. "Dennis "Is dad going to kill George down stairs for killing queenie? "Nana "No Dennis we don't know if he did it so nothing can be done and you must not say anything to him, let your dad and mum sort it out. "Mel "I know it was him I just know it was, he is a mean man and I hope he dies soon. "Nan "And so do we all Mel. Right let's get you home after wiping all that ice cream off your chops."

Well things were not the same in the house after what happened to our beautiful dog queenie and Den seemed very lost without her, how could anyone do such a thing something so cruel and vindictive? Dad never forgot what had happened and if left to his own devices he would have probably ended up in prison for murder. Mum was lost without queenie as she was a constant companion to her at all times and now even that was taken away, it was a cruel time in this troubled world, the war was over but meanness still existed with close neighbours who once stood together against tyranny and some never came out of it with a clear conscience. It took a lot of courage to hang on to her sanity in the situation mum was in and she could not wait to get out of that valley and often considered heading home to her mums for a while. She came from a peaceful quiet family and she was not used to this reaction from people, she lived only about 12 miles from there and often commented it was a different world and had she had her way she would be back home in her village of Pencoed, you could tell she was missing her old way of life and I think if they had gone back there mum would have had a happier life.

As things stood it was a hard time but the day finally came and off to a new life. The council stuck by their word and mum and dad was one of the first ones of 4 families to move into this new village that was being created.

CHAPTER 2

IT CAME FROM NOWHERE.

Well it was amazing there was a new village being created from nothing and we were the first to experience it. We had no choice as to where we were going to live; it was decided for us, why? Because it was to do with the way the village was laid out. We went to the main street going like a horse shoe around the top of this huge mountain and that street was going to determine the rest of the site and no 51 Heol Glannant, Bettws, was where the major bend was in the street and give the site its direction in fact it was 4 houses that decided this no45 to 51 and it had the only definite corners in that street the rest of it went around like a horse shoe and you could see the shape of the place if you went up to the top of the mountain above the village and looked down. From the village we could see the sea and at night the light house flashing in Porthcawl around 12 miles away but the wind didn't half whistle around there it was open to all the elements, but mum and dad didn't care it was a new start.

Well it happened on the 3rd of April 1954 I was born in the new posh Bridgend General Hospital and things went well at first but on the day I was one of twins and she did not make it, she was born and within a few minutes she died, the doctors said she was under nourished because I had consumed most of what my mother had eaten an so she was too weak to survive or was this another problem caused by the arsenal which affected my mother's health. Well they named me Daniel and I was born perfect no problems with my eyes and nothing that was visible, mum and dad was delighted and I was one of the first babies to be born to Bettws and one of the first to experience the awful weather in winter that was so cold.

Bettws was like a large meccano set the houses were brought in on the back of lorries in large concrete and steel slabs and bolted together in place and the floors were put in and the roof trusses put on and tiled then they were then sprayed in a cement stipple and painted white some of these houses were erected in a matter of 5 to 7 days it was the inside that took the time. There was not any central heating just a fire place in the 2 downstairs rooms they would prove to be very cold to live in and the pipes would freeze in the winter, but the whole reason for these houses was due to the war, there was a shortage of houses and they were designed to be erected fast and replaced in 20 years just to accommodate thousands of people as soon as possible. Well it was like a huge playground for me and Den as there was no cars not even a proper road for many years to come.

I will pick up my story from when I could remember. It was around the age of 3 or 4 and I remember all the tumps of earth outside the houses and hardly many houses were actually finished. My first recollection was about half a dozen of us playing outside on the tumps, things like cowboys and

Indians. I remember Wyndham Pit who in years to come would be my best friend for many years. He was a year older than me and had little round glasses and looked exactly like the Milky bar kid off the TV adverts and everyone said so he was a good friend and a bit mischievous and did not suffer fools at all, next there was the Pothecary family and Potter was my age and in my opinion a little strange and laughed at anything but a nice person, then there was Alan Kendall he was a quiet lad and was always laughing and liked a bit of fun we were like mad kids and they never said much about Dennis and got on with him ok but was very wary about him. I remember many days of fun and Den and I were always dirty due to the mud everywhere, I remember many workmen everywhere in Bettws with roll up cigarettes in their mouths and one day I was shocked by what happened.

We were all sitting around one day and Wyndham was out with his latest thing, I spoke to him "What have you got there?" Wyndham said "My mum went to Bridgend and bought a bubble pipe, I am a smoker now" at that he blew into it and loads of bubbles flew out of its Den was amazed but weary of this and said "Oh look at that what is it?" Wyndham said "What did he say?" I said "He wants to know what it is, I don't think he has ever seen something like that, mind you neither have I." Wyndham said "Brilliant isn't it, I never saw one until my mum got it from Bridgend. She got 3 of them for me, I think it is brilliant but I am going to smoke it for real tonight." Next thing Potter said "How do you mean? You haven't got any tobacco." Wyndham said "No but your dad smokes a pipe, don't he?" Potter replies "Yes but it's bigger than that one." Wyndham said "Well he won't miss a little tobacco, then will he?" Potter looking worried said "He will kill me if he caught me." Wyndham spoke and said "No he won't don't be silly you will never get caught." Potter just looked at him and then with a big smile he said "Why not I will get some and we will hide behind the tumps and have a smoke, I will see you later." He ran off pleased with himself and Den chirped up "That's naughty, I will tell your father." Wyndham said "What did he say?" I said "He is going to tell your father." Wyndham says "Will he? I will hit him if he does. "I replied "Then we will both have to hit you first wont we?" Wyndham "Yeah and I will get my big brother on you then." Den started to bite his fist and growl at Wyndham and he looked frightened and said "I don't like him he is nuts, will he hit me?" I said "Yes if I tell him to, no he is harmless but he won't tell your dad if I tell him not to. I think that Potter will turn up with lots of tobacco tonight but where will you get matches from?" Wyndham "I can get them easy my dad and mum smoke so I will nick some from them and we can build a fire and pretend we are Indians."

Well it was later on that evening that we met up around the corner and we lit a small fire and sat around the fire and Potter give us some tobacco and we watched as Wyndham filled this plastic pipe up and was ready for the big smoke, this pipe was not like plastic now, in them days plastic was thicker and harder and it would take a long time for it to eventually melt and we would have a big shock when it did. Wyndham grabbed the pipe and said "Well here goes, I am going to light it, you lot keep a look out." He lit the pipe and he started to cough his guts out in between coughs he said "Oh my god this isn't bad, anyone else want a try?" No one said anything but Dennis was smiling as if to say I will have a go but like a fool I said I would and he passed the pipe to me, I took a small drag from it and started to cough violently and Wyndham and I were grey in the face and laughing then Potter had a go, he coughed and went blue then the pipe went out the tobacco was all gone and we were laughing and Wyndham said to Potter "Give me some more tobacco." Potter said "I haven't got any more I could only get that amount, he hardly had any." Wyndham "Well what are we going to do now?" I said "Let's split up and the workmen and other people drop their fag ends everywhere and we can get them and get the tobacco out and use that." Potter said "Good idea, we will go up the hill and you go down towards the bottom." Off we went and collected the fag ends and got out the tobacco and put it into the pipe not realising it was not pipe tobacco and it would burn even hotter and this pipe was about to meet it's end with almost tragic circumstances for Dennis.

Well Wyndham lit it up again and I had a drag and everyone else except Dennis and he was smiling as if to say give me a go. Wyndham spoke to him "Do you want a drag Den?" Den nodded and Wyndham gave him the pipe, Den took a drag and all of a sudden, he stood up dead straight and proceeded to cough violently until he was almost not breathing, I panicked and tried to help him and we all panicked, I was slapping him on the back and he was still not breathing properly. I was by this time crying and did not know what to do, Potter pulled out a bottle of water and offered it to Den and he had a small dribble of it and started to breathe but hardly at all at first until after about 3 minutes he was back to normal. I realise now what had happened because of the problem with Dennis's mouth he could not breathe like anyone else and that tobacco could have killed him. I realise now we could have killed him so I never let him try it again. Well later on in the night we lit it up again and Wyndham looked professional by now but he went a little too far and he had the pipe between his thumb and fore finger and the plastic melted onto his hand, I never seen anyone jump so much and he was running all over the place screaming and we were all killing ourselves laughing.

Later that night we went home and we got into the house and I was still laughing and mum said "What's so funny Danny boy?" I replied "Oh nothing." Not wanting them to find out about the pipe and then out of the blue Dennis chirps up and said "We were laughing at Wyndham smoking that pipe and he burnt himself." Dad says "What's this about a pipe?" I quickly tried to cover up and said "Oh Wyndham was pretending to smoke a pipe, one of those bubble ones from Woolworths." Dad said "So how did he burn himself? "I said "No he was pretending." Next thing Den spoke up again "And I nearly choked and Danny was being sick too." Dad looked at me and I knew then he didn't believe me and he said "I think you and

Dennis should take me to the camp fire now." He hooked me and den out and Den took dad straight to the spot and when we got there, there was no hiding the fact that we had been smoking, loads of fag ends a melted plastic pipe and remains of a fire. I went home and off to bed and kept in for a week, my dad went and told all the other parents and I was labelled a grass all because of Dennis he could not help but to tell the truth, I realised from then on If I was going to have a little fun behind my parents back, I was going to have to leave Dennis out.

It was a few weeks later that the lads started talking to me again thanks to Den and Den would keep on reminding me that he was watching me so I had better behave myself. He would get into an older brother mood as if to say he was in charge and look at me I am grown up, I somehow had to find a way around his type of blackmailing. Well the roads started to get finished and we found we had a large green outside our house like a football pitch and in time it would be known as Ducko park and we would play football and cricket on it and it would bring all the neighbours children together in competition and a major meeting point in our little zone and caused some problems sometimes as the ball was not always given back for a few days if it went into someone's garden too many times and dad was one of the worst ones as he grew vegetables in every garden even in the front gardens, not lawns but vegetables he said we can't eat grass so in a way he was right.

My older brother was a close friend to a family opposite to us named the Webster's and they were a lovely family and treated Den like an old friend and he loved it, we had many times a good reason to laugh with them as the boys were so funny and got up to lots of mischief, one day we saw old man Webster tie a cow to his washing line post because it broke through his rear fence to eat his vegetables and so he tied it to a sturdy line post and was going to keep it until the farmer came to collect it and get the money off the farmer, Den and I was fascinated by this animal and watched it all day and when it came to Milking time the cow just got up and walked away bending the line post over until the rope holding it just slipped off the top and it trundled off to milking and Mr Webster just stood there in amazement and never got his compensation. On another occasion Mel, Mike Webster Brian Webster, and Derek Webster would pretend to be firemen and would start a little fire in the corner of the wooden shed in their garden and run and get buckets of water and a hose pipe and put it out, Den would be tickled to death with these doing this and used to laugh, until one day they set a little fire in the usual place in the shed and said leave it a little longer to make it harder and so they did they then proceeded to fetch water to put it out but had left it a little too long and they could not put it out and it was well alight and the fire brigade had to be called out, it was so funny but the boys were not laughing and scattered everywhere. Well the fire engine arrived and the sirens were wailing and next thing Den heard this sound and got frightened and run inside the garden of our house, he was amazed and he was so fascinated by this big large truck the day was born when he had an incredible love for lorries and was always keeping on about them, well the shed burnt down and Mel and the Webster's got into hot water for a long time but Dennis just kept on about the fire engine I used to fancy Anne Webster very much and Dennis used to say I will tell her you love her and I would threaten Dennis but I still love Anne to this day..

Well xmas came that year and we had a huge shock Den and I had a 3-wheeler bike each for xmas and was the only boys on the road to have one each, we had a brilliant xmas that year as were most Christmases we had. Den loved his bike which was bigger than mine and looked very flashy, he however would let friends have a go at any time but would fuss over keeping it clean and ride it slowly, he had a little saddle bag on the back which he kept a couple of coppers in to make him feel like a grown up.

Well there was this day he was called in to get dressed up and I was taken up to Nans for the day as yes you guessed it Den's trip to Hensel had come again and all hell was about to break loose, this you could see in my mother's face. Well Den got ready and thought he was going shopping or up to see Nan. They got into the sidecar of the motor bike and off they went, it was a day they will remember as Den was much older now and a larger lad with incredible strength and as they approached Hensel Castle, he tried to make a break for it and dad almost crashed the motorbike. He had to stop and Den said "I want to go home; I am not going in there no, no, no." Dad grabbed Den by the wrists and tried to calm him down "Ok Den it's not a problem, we are not staying we are only going in for a minute or two. "Mum crying said "C'mon Den we will stay with you, no one is going to hurt you if we go in now, we can get home quickly ok?" Den was still struggling with dad and said "You promised I am not coming here again, I'm running home to tell Nan about you. "Dad said "Now don't be silly, we must do this or they will take you away from us and you will never see us again." Hearing that Den got worse and was by now almost out of the sidecar and crying "No, no I am off I don't want to go in there. "Mum by now was in serious tears and dad frustrated shouted out loud at Dennis "Stop it, stop it, or I will smack you hard. "He proceeded to shake Dennis and Den stopped and started sobbing uncontrollably, dad got off the bike left it there and took Den into the hospital by his arm. Den still sobbing and mum left by the bike sobbing uncontrollably too. People were staring at them and Den and dad disappeared into the hospital, it was a few minutes later that dad came out to comfort mum. Dad said "Are you allright Eileen? I am sorry but I had to do that he was out of control and I was afraid what was going to happen." Mum looks at dad as if to say you should not have done that, she then said "That will stay with me for the rest of my life, he is our son not some lunatic, are you starting to believe what they are all saying? Because that was not the way to treat him." Dad with head bowed said "Yes I know I am sorry. "Mum says "Save your apologies for that boy and hope he will except it, where is he now and what's happening?" Dad replies "He is being calmed down by the nurses before he goes in to see the doctor, I came out to see how you are. "Mum says "I think you should have stayed with him he is the one who is frightened." Mum storms off and blanks dad as she went into the hospital, dad follows.

Inside and Den was still crying but not so much and he lunged out of the nurse's hands and went straight to mum who had now stopped crying. Den said to her "Can we go now mum?" Mum sat on a chair and said to him "Den we have got to do this but I shall come in with you this time. "Dad chirped up "And so will I, I won't leave you here. "Den still crying says "Then can we go? "Mum said "Yes, I promise. "Dad says "Don't make promises we can't keep." Mum replies "I am going in with him, I don't know what you are doing but I am, I don't care what they say." Dad just shrugged his shoulders. Next, they were watching another little one sitting there very quiet and   Den tried to speak to her while holding the tears back" Hi, I am Dennis, I am a fireman what's your name?" The little girl just sat there not answering and Den looked at mam and said "I think she is nuts like me." That broke the ice and they all started laughing, just then a nurse called out "Dennis Duckfield." Dad says "Here. "The nurse comes over and goes to grab Dennis by the hand and mum said "I will fetch him in with me. "The nurse replies "Sorry you will have to wait here, only the patient please. "Mum looked at her very sternly and said "He is not going in there without me, I don't care what you say." The older nurse in a blunt voice says "I am sorry that is impossible, the doctor just wants Dennis." Mum replies "Well he is not going to get Dennis without me, got it? "The nurse said "This is irregular, I am sorry I will have to go and speak to the doctor first." Mum replies "Well go ahead then." The nurse storms off and dad says to mum "Oh don't start a fuss now, we don't want to have to come back again in the future, it will not do Den any good at all." Mum says "I don't give a shit. I am fed up of everyone telling me what is the best for my son, its time I spoke up, he is not going anywhere without me, got it?" Dad rolls his eyes and says "Ok, ok." The nurse returns and says to mum "The doctor says he must see Dennis on his own and that you will just distract him, Dennis that is, so please let me have him and you sit there with your husband and we shall not be long." Mum standing her ground and dad looking flustered says "He is not going anywhere without me, what don't you understand about that sentence?" The nurse turns and looks at dad and he just shrugs his shoulders. The nurse turns back to mum and say "Right wait a minute. "She storms off and returns and says "Very well, follow me. "Mum with a smile as if to say I have won says "Lead the way and I shall follow. "Off they go and dad just sat there probably feeling stupid.

Den and mum enter the doctor's room and immediately the doctor starts on mum and the nurse has a smile on her face as they set to it, the doctor says "I am sorry you need to be in here as I am doing things with Den. Can you tell me why?" Mum looking sheepish speaks "Why shouldn't I be in here with Den? He is my son and he is very upset." Doctor replies "This is very irregular and off putting for him though isn't it?" Mum says in reply "Well I am sorry doctor but that is how it is going to be." The doctor snaps at mum "Its mister not doctor, I have earned this title, I am a professor not a doctor I am Mr Hughes not doctor, and I would be glad if you could remember that." Mum says "So you are Mr Hughes are you? well we meet at last, you seem to be so cock sure of yourself don't you and you seem to know my boy better than me according to your letter, well let me tell you something Mr Hughes I am Mrs Duckfield to you I am not some dimwit from the valleys you can shove from pillar to post, so get off your high horse and do your job and have a look at my son, or would you want to have your Hench woman over there try and throw me out because I am interested in my sons welfare." The professor was sitting there dumfounded and said "Ok let's start again, I think we have got off on the wrong foot." Mum says "There's no we, you have started this not me I just want to have my input into my sons future and not be treated as if me and my husband don't exist in this." The professor looking nervous says "That will be all nurse I can manage now." The nurse looks at the doctor as if to say you should be sending her out not me storms out of the room and the professor continues to speak "Hello Dennis how are you then? It's nice that you have brought your mummy, can we have a little play with these coloured blocks? Perhaps mummy can help us. "Back outside in the waiting room dad is sitting there for some 2 hours waiting for mum and she and Den appears with the consultant all smiling. She shakes his hand and says goodbye and walks up to dad, he says "Everything ok then? "Mum replies "Of course, why shouldn't it be? Or were you hoping he was staying?" Dad looking upset says "Oh don't be like that Eileen, I am sorry let's have a cup of tea before we leave. "Den starts to panic "No, no let's go, I want to go home and go out too play. "Dad says "Ok." Mum interrupts "Dennis you are not having it all your way we are having a cup of tea before we go and that's final. "She looks at Den as if to say, I am serious so don't go there. Den whispers" Oh allright then. "Dad laughs and off they go. They sit in a little café in the hospital and mum is explaining to dad expressing herself in a madamish manner "Yes I put him right, he thinks he is some type of god and so does that bloody nurse, nan would be proud of me, anyway Den has improved a tiny bit nothing to get excited about but he is happy with him and wants to see him in 3 years." Den says "No I am not coming back here again, I am not." Dad says "Ok, ok, let's leave it there until we get home and the boys are in bed." And so off they set for home.

It was the next day and things were a little raw still with mum and dad but Dennis was back to himself. Mum seemed to have got a little harder from that hospital visit and lost patience with people and tried to avoid confrontation and she started sticking up for her sons more and more, this was not a bad thing. But for Dennis things were up and down he was growing up and no one knew how his teenage years were going to be, it is hard enough for a normal teenager to get through so how is this going to affect him. Well things with him was starting to get worse and worse. The following year his incontinence got worse, he was out on his bike with me one day and it happened again, one of the local kids wanted ago on his bike and Den said he can but the lad was in such a hurry he did not notice that Dennis had fouled the seat and the kid just sat right in it the kid in amongst all the crowd screams and starts crying "Oh no, oh no, I am going to be sick, Ah its everywhere." And all the kids around Den starts making sickly noises and they all started making fun at Dennis, this was the beginning of more troubles for mum dad, Dennis, Mel and myself. This village had grown up rapidly and was now a large melting pot of over a thousand people from all different valleys and cultures and we all very much lived on top of each other. Gossip was a big thing here and many people were placed here from their own village because they were unable to get on with their neighbours where they were from it was a place ready to irrupt at any time and Den was the perfect excuse as he was not a normal child.

Well after the event of the tricycle Den was left on his own for a long time no one wanted to play with him and he was made fun of by all the kids on the estate and many of the teenagers and even older ones, I am afraid I was as much to blame as I stayed well away from Dennis as it was easier for me to have friends as no one would have bothered with me with Den about and the girls were the cruellest of all. I was ashamed of Den but more ashamed of myself for feeling that way, so I just put up with it and got away from my street as often as I could.

Well this went on for a year or so and things started to settle down a bit and then I noticed other things happening to Den like he was conned into doing things by other boys and sometimes forced to do things that would get him into trouble and the kids would just laugh and run away while Den was kept in many times and you could see him many times in the bedroom window looking upset and wondering why the other kids who made him do these things were still out playing and he was not allowed. I used to get emotional about the things they did but did nothing about it, I remember one day we were playing cricket outside on Ducko park and we made Dennis stand right down the bottom of the hill to retrieve the ball and make him do all the running which he loved for about half an hour but soon got fed up with it and when he did I would threaten him with Hensel Castle if he wouldn't do it so he did. Well one day he had his own back he had incredible strength and he could hurl a ball like a rocket at great speed and I was batting and I hit the ball and it went straight past Dennis and as the ball headed for Dennis he went down on his hands and knees and put his hands over his head to shield himself as he was afraid of the ball and I started to make runs, all the boys were shouting at him to get the ball quickly and throw it back he was in a real foul mood at this and grabbed the ball and threw it at a tremendous pace it hit the nearest wicket to the bowler and snapped it in half it then hit me full on the foot and I went down like a shot elephant and I was in agony my foot went up like a balloon and I was writhing in agony after a while I looked up and Dennis was still at the bottom of the road and he was laughing his head off and slapping his hands together as If to say that will teach you to shout at me. Well I never saw the rest of the match I was in the house for a week with my foot up in agony.

Dennis was growing up at a fast pace by now as was I and also the village that we lived in, I remember how mum started to go on the bus every Saturday to her mothers and sisters in Pencoed and she used to take me and Dennis with her, we always looked forward to this and this is when Den became a different lad, he just loved busses and in time he thought he was a bus and some funny things which will come up in the next few chapters but it was amazing how different Den was when he was on those busses he was so calm and watched everything the driver did and the bus conductor, he was mesmerised by it he also loved it in Pencoed where my nan and granddad lived on what they called the green a huge circular green outside my nans and granddad. At my grandad he grew gooseberries in the garden and we would pick loads for mam to take home and we could eat as many as we liked and Den stuffed himself until he had a bad stomached then we would pick some rhubarb which was huge and if there was anything under the leaves a spider or a frog or anything, Den was running like the wind to get away from it so we used to send him out to pick it and watch and wait to see this. After a few hours in Nan's we would go down aunty Mabel's to see the family, have some tea there and see our cousins and then up to see uncle Leighton and Alma. Well they lived alongside the main railway line to London and Den and I used to watch the trains go bye, this was a treat for us and Den and I. I remember Den and I felt so calm and down there it was such a pleasant place to be, no one made fun of Dennis and we made friends with many children there and they would not make fun and now I could see what mum meant when she always said I wish I was in Pencoed it is nicer there and no hassles. She was right we would have had a nicer life there as Den's life would run smoother but it was not to be so back to hell every Saturday evening and a quiet Sunday at home.

It was when Den was about 10 or 11 years of age that things started to get a little hairy for no reason as Den never had a nasty bone in his body but many people would make out that it is not so, well a new neighbour moved into the village and they had a little girl named Alison who was a lovely little girl about the same age as Den, she was a little quiet and a little slow in the way she was a little like Den and Den and her got very friendly although the mother was very cautious about it and that soon subsided when she could see that they both loved it in their own little world and played happily as long as they were left alone and they were always in sight of each other. Den said to her one day "Do you like music? "Alison replies with a lovely smile "Yes do you? Den. "Den smiles back and says "Yes, I do, I can play drums you know. "Alison says "I can play the guitar, we can play together." Den says "Yes have you seen this, I have got a sherbet dip. "Alison "Have you, can I have a look?" Den shows her and she says "My mummy can't afford any sweets for me so I can't have any." Den his face lights up and he says "You can share mine. "Alison's face lights up and she says "Thanks

Dennis and if my mummy buys me any sweets in the week, I will share them with you." Next thing Den opens the sherbet and takes out the lolly and gives her the bag of sherbet and sticks the lolly in his mouth Den says "There you go then that's for you." She grabs the bag of sherbet and wonders what to do with it then she rips the top off and takes a mouthful she screws up her face and coughs, Den looks at her and says "I know it's awful isn't it? I don't like the sherbet its bitter, do you like it? "Alison face still screwed up says "Aw its allright I suppose, are you my best friend Den? "Den looking puzzled says "Of course I am your boyfriend, aren't I? "Alison "Are you? I like to have a boyfriend, does that mean you are going to marry me? "Den laughs and says "Don't be silly I have got to get a job yet, I am going to drive busses." Alison then says "I like bus conductors I do, are you going to do that too?" Den "Oh yes of course, I had better get home and sort out my washing things to clean my bus before it gets dark." Alison "Ok see you later if you like. "Den "Yes ok I will as soon as I have finished washing my bus." Den left and Alison sat on her own and next thing a group of girls surrounded her and started saying bad things to her. The 1st girl said to Alison "You got a boyfriend, Dennis duck, haven't you?" Alison just sat their head bowed and looked as if she was about to cry. 1st girl speaks again "She is like Dennis, she is stupid and Dennis poo's his pants and smells I can smell he has been here or is it you? "Alison starts crying and is frightened. 2nd girl "Oh little cry baby, cry baby, my mother says you and Dennis are mad so stay away from us and tell Dennis we think he is mad and if you know what is good for you, you will stay away from him and off the street because we don't like you at all." Next thing a shout from afar "Alison, Alison come on time for tea. "The girls run away and Alison is left there on her own crying. Her mother comes over to where she is and asks "What's the matter my darling? Were those girls picking on you?" Alison cry's even more and wraps her arms around her mother and sobs, her mother comforts her saying "There, there, there, no one's going to hurt you, I will sort this out, c'mon stop crying I don't like to see you like this, tell me what happened." Alison composers herself and says "They said I was mad and so was Dennis and I had better be careful or else." Her mum says "Or else what? I will sort this out, has Dennis done anything? "Alison still crying snaps "No, no, he is nice, he went home to clean his bus." Her mum starts laughing and Alison starts laughing at her mum and her mum says "Dennis has a bus, oh god I will start walking if he has a bus. "

Back in the house and Den was eating his tea and says to mum "Can I go back out I have to meet my girlfriend. "Mum looks amazed and says "Who's your girlfriend? "Den "You know. "Mum "No I don't, who is she then.?" Den goes a little red and starts laughing and says "You know Alison she has been my girlfriend for ages, we might be getting married if I get a job." Mum giggles and dad looking stern said "Well I hope you are behaving yourself, I am not sure you should be hanging out with girls, she is younger than you I hope you are not messing with her, I think you had better stay away from her before there is trouble." Den's face dropped and he went serous and looked upset and said "Aw its allright we are good friends, she is my best friend and not yours so don't say things." Dad "What did you say? I will give you, I think you had better get up to your bedroom mate." Den loses his temper and bites his fist and snarls at dad "You mind your own business she's my friend." Dad snaps "Right up to your bedroom." Next mum intervenes "Why are you treating him like this ray he has not done anything wrong." Den says "Yes I have been good." Mum again "That boy can't do anything, you just think he is some sort of pervert all the time, leave him alone for goodness sake." Dad in nasty tone "He is not hanging around with little girls in this village you know what people are like here, he will be accused of molesting them, best to keep him in for a day or two." Mum "I don't believe my ears, you are as sick as the people who say these things ,you may as well lock him up and throw away the key, why not leave the boy alone and worry about your bloody rabbits." Dad "Yeh, Yeh, just remember I said this." Dad storms out of the house and Den looks at mum and says "He's a horrible man I like Alison and we are friends, can I go out now?" Mum says "I hope you are being good with Alison, are you?" Den "Yes. "Mum "Ok then but you must be in as soon as the street lights come on ok? "Den rubs his hands together and with huge smile says "Ok I will see you. "Den runs out and after that day mum and dad didn't speak for a few days and you could feel the tension in the air. Den in the meantime went looking for Alison that evening but she was not out and Den would not knock the door so he was very disappointed and I think he thought dad had something to do with it, Den was alone again sitting in the grass on Ducko park he always looked like he wanted to have just one good mate but all he got is youngsters passing bye him either ignoring him, laughing at him or making jibes at him. He could not win and I think he just got used to it at that age.

Well it was the next day and Den was out alone on the grass again and he was waiting for Alison to come home from school and she passed him and said nothing and just went in never looked at Den and went straight in the house. Den shouted to her "Hi Alison are you coming out to play? I will Waite here until you have had your tea. "She just ignored him, I think she was worried about what the other girls had said to her. Well Den went in for his tea and sat at the table looking as if he had lost a hundred pounds. Mum said "What's the matter Den? "Den "Him. "Pointing at dad. Mam said "What has dad done? "Den looking nasty says "He stopped Alison playing with me, she won't speak to me now. "Mum smiles and says "I don't think so, dad has not said anything have you? "Looking at dad who says "No." Mum says "There, I told you, I expect she is just being shy, maybe she will be out after and you can ask her. "Dad said "Or maybe her mother has warned her too. "Mum "Aw shut up and grow up. "Dad went silent again. Mum put her arm around Den and said "Guess what I made today Den? "Den playing with mum "Ah cakes, ah welsh cakes. "Mum "How do you know? "Den smiles and replies "Because I can smell them. "Mum and Den shouted "Yes." Den "Can I take some to Alison? "Mum smiles back and says "Of course you can but put them in a piece of greaseproof paper not in your pocket. "Den wrapped 2 in paper 2 in his hands for him and stuffed the cakes in the paper in his pocket and off he went.

Den went off to look for Alison and was disappointed yet again when she was not there. I went out behind him and he was sitting on the grass looking down and muttering to himself, I spoke to him "Allright Den what's the matter?" I looked at him and he smiled and said "Oh nothing I am waiting for my girlfriend she is having food, she won't be long." I said "She will be out now, see you later Den." Den "Where are you going? "Dan "I am going to look for the boys. "Den excited "Can I come? "Dan "No I am going to be a long time and dad will be looking for you. "This was a lie as I didn't want him with me. Den said "Oh ok. "I walked off and Den started muttering again, I felt sorry for him as he was in the street all alone and he was looking lost, well I went around the corner and I saw Alison with some girls and that made me feel worse, she had forgotten about Dennis and found new friends or so I thought. One of the girls said to me "Your Dennis ducks' brother, aren't you? "I said "No I am Dennis Duckfield brother not duck. "She laughed and said" He is a nutter and Alison has finished with him and he pooh's himself, he is a pig." In the corner of my eye I could see Alison and she looked a frightened girl, I said to the girl "You are a horrible girl, aren't you? Go home and have a wash, I can smell you from here. "She replied "Look at yourself dirty knees and dirty hair I am going to tell my mother about you. "I said "I don't care, Alison Den is waiting for you he thinks you are going out to play with him. "Alison looked at me and nodded no, I just walked on. This made me feel worse so I found my mates but it was no use I felt awful and went back to find Den and yes there he was still sitting there. I said to him "Still here then Den? Fancy a game of football?" Den "No I can't play football I don't think." Dan "Yes you can, I will teach you it's easy." I ran and got the ball and we started to get sorted out, I said to Den "Right c'mon stand up and I will kick the ball to you and you must kick it back." He stood up reluctantly and I kicked the ball to him and I have never seen anyone so awkward in my life he had no clue, he seemed afraid of the ball and so I said in a playful manner to encourage him "Go on Den get the ball and kick it back." He smiled and picked up the ball and placed it on a spot so as it would not run down the hill and walked back a few paces and run and kicked it, it went totally the wrong way and sent me running after it. Den in the meantime was laughing and slapping his hands together and so excited I shouted "Steady where are you kicking it? I am over here not over there." Den laughed even more and was getting more and more excited I had never seen him laugh so much, I kicked it back he run after it and done the same again and this time he was shouting "Look out its coming get it." And he was laughing some more, well this went on for a half hour and I was puffing and panting but then the lads turned up and I just stopped and went to the boys after a few minutes I looked around and Dennis had gone in I remember feeling a right waster, my own brother and I was treating him like a nobody.

Well a few days went bye it had rained for those days and Dennis was stuck in the house and did not see Alison or anyone else for that matter and then I was walking home from school and in the distance from my house I could see a commotion. It was Dennis and the bully girls picking on him, I for the first time shouted at them and they scattered, when I got up to Dennis, he was picking up stuff off the road he had got up the shop for mum, I said to Den "What are you doing? "Den replied "I was giving them my sweets." Dan "Why?" Den "They said they would tell Alison to meet me if I gave them my sweets." Dan "The little cows and did you give them all of them ?" Den "Yeh they like me I said I will meet them later and bring more sweets." Dan said in sad voice "Den their lying, they just want your sweets." Den all smiles says "They are my new friends." Dan trying to convince Den says "No their not they just want your sweets honestly." Den in a moody voice "No their not, I am telling mammy." Den just run off and I followed him into the house he was telling mum and mum started shouting at me "What are you doing to him again?" Dan said "Nothing mum he gave his sweets to some horrible girls and he is going to do it again, they are just after his sweets." Mum looks at Dennis he smirks and she says to him "Den you haven't give them your sweets, oh my goodness I'll give you I cannot afford to buy you sweets for you to give them away you're a naughty boy and you had better stay in until your father gets home." Den starts biting his fist and stares nasty at me and says "It's you, I am telling dad and you will be in trouble, go away. " I said "Don't you bite your fist at me or I will wack you one." I grabbed him by the arm and we grappled Den in a very nervous manner, mum screamed "Right stop it, stop it, you get over there and Den you get over there." I stormed off to get changed and had my tea and went out, Dennis all the time muttering about me well I went down the road and I saw the girls who had taken Dens sweets and they ran into one of their gardens and shouting at me but I couldn't care less after the way Den started on me, little did I know this was the only way Den could be in his mind he was most certainly different from all other people, but things were getting worse for me because of Dennis's problems. He stood out like a sore thumb, there was no hiding him.

Yes, the inevitable happened and it was not nice as it always ended up in Dennis getting the fault, well the bully girls were with Alison and keeping her from Dennis was their aim and they were good at it. Well Den caught sight of them and hid behind a van and was playing at being invisible until he decided he was going to pounce and make the girls jump, this was innocent to him but not to the girls. He was listening and the girls were singing a song called ring a ring roses and Den jumped out quickly and shouted "Hello it's me. "In a loud voice and the girls ran away screaming, he had definitely made them jump. Next thing one of the parents came out of their house and said to Den "You are a real asshole, aren't you? Does your mother and father know where you are and what you are doing?" Den smiling said "Yes I always play with the girls." The man replied "Not anymore mate, you leave them alone." Den said in an innocent voice "They are my friends." Man replies "I don't care you get down by your own house." Den just stood there and smiled as if he did not know what he was going on about, next the leader of the bully girls said "He won't leave Alison alone, he follows her and she is frightened of him aren't you?" Looking at Alison, Alison just stared at the road said nothing but started crying and the man said "Is that so we will see about this." He grabbed Den by the scruff and walked him onto Ducko park and said to him "Now you stay here and leave the girls alone ok." Den looked shocked and frightened and the bully girls laughing and said to the man "He will only come back." The man said out loud for Den to hear "He had better not or I will set the dog on him. "Den sat on the grass head in hands, this had frightened him and threatening to set the dog on him was no laughing matter as Den was petrified of strange dogs. The girls had won and they made fun of him even more.

Well it finally came to a head one day when Den was walking back from the shop and saw the bully girls and they were making fun at Alison and she was sobbing her eyes out and Den could hear everything they were saying and he snapped. Bully girl to Alison "Alison loves dirty Dennis duck and she smells like him. "Another girl was pushing Alison about. Den run up to them and this time they could not get away, he shouted "Don't do that to Alison she is my girlfriend and Alison she is crying. "Den then put his arm around Alison to sort of move her out of danger and the bully girls tried to escape but Den was too quick and they were cornered and the bully girls started crying. Den started shouting "I am going to tell your father I am and my mother and father, I hate you stupid girls. "By this time, they were all sobbing and parents started coming out and of course they would only see half of the story and it was nothing what had really happened. All they could see is four or five little girls crying and Dennis in the middle shouting. This was going to cause Den some trouble, well Alison's mother came out and took Alison away from Dennis and they went straight in, Den went home pronto smiling and as far as he was concerned it was nothing but this was going to be a long night.

It was one hour later and mum and Den was in the house and Den had said nothing. Next a knock on the door, mum went and opened it and there was 2 men standing there one of them spoke "Hello Mrs Duckfield we are here to complain about your boy Dennis he is making our girls lives hell and we have had enough. If you don't do something about it we will." mum looking shocked said "What are you talking about?" Second man "Well he attacked our girls who are crying out their in the house, he cornered them up by the phone box and started shouting at them like a maniac, this is bad and we will get him locked up if it happens again I assure you, you should keep him locked up." Mum says "I have no idea what you are talking about but I will speak to Dennis and when my husband comes home I shall send him up to see you about it." Well the men knowing dad was in work and didn't want to leave this go and went to say more but mum cut them short and said "Thank you good day." And shut the door. She went in to speak to Dennis before dad got home. Mum speaks to Dennis "What the hell have you done? "Den looked shocked and scratching his head and replied "Nothing I stopped the girls hitting Alison and making her cry." Mum "How did you do that? I hope you didn't hit any of them or your father will be very angry so tell me what did you do?" Den panicking says "Nothing I have not done anything, I never hit them they were hitting Alison that's all." Mum "I hope you are telling the truth because your dad has to go and see them later and if he finds out your telling lies he will not be very happy." Dennis starts to cry and mum says to him "Oh don't start crying, I am just fed up with it all, I never get a week go bye without there being any trouble." Next thing Dad walks in, he sees them both in a state and says "Right what's happened? I can see there is something wrong." Mum says "Ok keep your hair on, we don't know what has happened but the fella from up the road the one with those big dogs and another man came here to complain about Dennis and said that he made their girls cry and frightened them after cornering them by the telephone box, but don't take it out on Dennis until you have found out the truth." Dad looks at Dennis and says "So what have you done Den? Come on tell me I hope you have not touched any of those children, have you? "Den looks down to the ground and says "I stopped them hitting Alison that's all and they started screaming. "Dad "Oh dear I don't believe it, I hope that you are telling the truth, I am off to see that idiot. Den is to stay here. "Dad storms off and up to confronts the man who a few nights before dragged Den by the scruff but dad didn't know this. Dad knocks the door and the man answers. Dad says "You wanted to see me about my son Dennis?" Man says to dad "God you are as cantankerous as him, he has been hanging around the girls that's my girl and her friends and today he threatened them and scared them half to death. What are you going to do about it? "Dad looks at him and replies "What do you mean? They are kids and these things happen, he did not touch them he is not that type of boy and from what I can gather your daughter and her friends were bullying Alison and making her cry and that's why Dennis intervened, if they were behaving this would not have happened. "Man "So it's my daughters' fault is it? Well I think Alison's mother would not agree, your boy has been hanging around her too often lately and I wouldn't trust him with my dog, he is a danger to all the kids here." Dad said "He has not done anything so be careful what you are saying unless you can back it up or shut your mouth, I am not afraid of you or your dog's mate so stay away from my son unless you have any proof. I shall sort him out you sort your daughter out." Dad storms off and calls into see Alison's mother, he knocks the door and she answers "Oh hello Mr Duckfield I was expecting you, I don't know what happened I just know that Alison is very upset and I can't get a word out of her and I am not going to force it out of her but as soon as I get the truth out of her I will come and see you." Dad says "I would be very grateful if you would, I will keep Dennis away from her until we get the truth out. I feel Dennis is a little mischievous but I really don't think he would harm anyone, I will leave it at that and I am sorry about all this, goodbye." Dad walks off and at home he comes in and says to mum "I don't know what has happened but they as usual want to blame Dennis but I am not having any of it until I hear from Alison's mother as Alison is too upset at the moment to say anything, but Dennis is staying in here for a day or two until it is sorted out ok?" Mum agrees reluctantly as she knows the neighbours will be gossiping again.

Well Den stayed in as promised although he was not happy about this and dad never saw Alison's mother again and Den was taken ill with yellow jaundice and was kept in for more than two weeks as it was too risky to let him out. Eventually he was let out and immediately he made a b line for Alison's house and waited outside for 2 days and he was unaware where she was but he continued to wait. Then the man with the 2 dogs had the pleasure of coming across the road to tell him, Man speaks to Den "Why are you hanging around here every day? "As he smirked Den says "I am waiting for my girlfriend you know." Man, then says smiling "Who is that then Dennis? "Dennis also starts smiling and says "You know Alison who lives in there. "He points to the house. Man, sniggers even more and says "Well you will have a long wait she has moved down to Bridgend to get away from you. "Den smiling and looking a bit sad "No she is in the house you are telling lies. "Man snarls "She's gone why don't you listen?? She has gone away and she is never coming back, so stop standing around here and go home you idiot and take that smell with you. "By this time Den's face was looking so down and he was getting nasty and says. "I am not listening to you so go away and leave me alone, I will tell my father about you he will sort you out." Man says "I'd like to see him try, now go down by your own house." Den was now biting his fist and showing his other fist to the man and starts shouting "Get away I hate you, I am waiting for Alison go away." Now speaking in tears next thing the man grabs Dennis by the arm and drags him down the street and dumps him on the grass. As he did my dad was coming down the hill. Dad jumps off the motorbike and grabs the man as Den was crying on the floor. Dad pushes him against the wall and said "Ok matey have a go at me, I am not someone you can push around easily, come on try it with me. "Dad was red in the face and the man looked worried and says "What's the matter with you man? I was just seeing him over the road, your nuts. "Dad still fuming says "Nuts, am I? I am fed up with the likes of you treating my family as if we came off another planet. "Den shouts over his tears "He sent Alison away and told me I am never to see her again. Dad beat him up. "Dad still steaming says to the man "Oh you did, did you? Aren't you brave? So, come on have a go at me now come on." Dad stood there and the man stood up straight and dad waited the man replies with childish voice. "No. "Dad then says "I thought not, but I'm telling you if you ever put a hand on my son again or speak to him in any nasty way, I am coming looking for you and next time I will not give you a second chance because I will put you in the hospital, now bugger off before I lose my temper." The man moves off quickly and dad goes over to Dennis and he was sobbing his heart out and dad comforts him "C'mon Den he will never touch you again I promise you." Den "I want Alison though she is my friend and she is the only one who plays with me." Dad looks sadly at Dennis and says "I know I am sorry but she had to move because of the girls making fun of her all time and her mother can't take no more of it and you will make more friends I'm sure, a nice lad like you, so jump up and we will go and wash my motorbike ok?" Dens face lit up and he said "I bags using the hose pipe then." Dad smiles and says "Ok then I'll race you." They run off down the road dad hanging back for Den to win.

Well soon came Christmas and we had some great presents and some fruit in our stockings. We also went to the Xmas party at the power station where dad worked. I had a huge rocket and a confectionary box Den had cars and a little garage and his confectionary box Mel had some tokens for some music albums and of course his confectionary box, little did we know that it would be our last xmas ever in our family and it was even our last birthday celebration life from now on was about to take a serious turn for the worse and this was about to affect our lives forever.

Chapter 3

Dad got religion.

Well it was the crazy 60's and everything was happening phsycadelia the Beatles and love what a great time it was everyone was so happy Mel and I were enjoying the Beatles era and buddy holly the beach boys and then. Mel turned out to be a genius and went to the Grammar school in Pontycymmer and he was one of a few who did in Bettws and we all laughed when he put on his grammar school uniform it was brown and had yellow trims around it but who cares when he had such a brilliant brain. Den was around a year younger than Mel and had no education at all such was the ways of the world towards people like Den and then there was our newest edition to the family baby Lyndon born in 1961 and was born with a harelip just like Dennis but was as normal as me and Mel.

It was on a lovely night in June the nineteenth to be exact Den and I was out on the front green late at night and I remember it was lovely and warm and we were kept out later than usual as the midwife had come to help mum with getting Lyndon to come in to this world. Well it was a lot of fun staying out so late and it was around 10, o'clock Lyndon was born and we were all so excited to know he was born almost perfect and we had a new young baby brother and Den was rubbing his hands together and got very excited and emotional.

It was one evening a man tall with a briefcase well-spoken hair growing out of his nose his ears and thick eyebrows knocked on our door to talk to anyone who would listen to him about his god who he named as Jehovah and dad stood there and listened, he even let him in our house, little did I know this was the end of my life as I knew it and darker times were ahead for us as a family.

Until my father took up the belief of religion, I hardly noticed he was there. He would sit down after coming home from work see to his animals his rabbits his chickens and sort his vegetable gardens out and he loved this then he would settle down and watch television programmes like Bonanza wagon train and rawhide and us children would be out playing and when it was dark watch telly or play with our train sets or many other things with mum. Those days we made our own fun, there was lots of fun in our household and mum always had a smile on her face which was a warm and loving smile and dad had a wicked smile and would tease us most of the time he would throw us up in the air and catch us, it was fun growing up in such a loving home. This man I spoke about earlier then started coming into our house in the evening at least once a week and he had a book he would quote from to us. Next thing I knew we all had a book each and we had to read a paragraph each and explain to each other what the meaning of this paragraph was all about, I remember the day of the week,

Wednesday I know this because I would be out playing with my friends, he would turn up and everything stopped with our family and we would have to sit down and do this whether we liked it or not because dad spoke and that is how it was going to be from now on and my friends did not matter anymore this man was more important than anything else, we as a family had to do was this Jehovah, or the King of England? he seemed to my father so very important. , Well it didn't end there it got worse and worse.

It was a Wednesday evening Den was playing and I was out with the boys and it was reasonably early, next we heard dad shouting "Dennis, Danny come on in its time c'mon." I ran in but Dennis stayed out not listening to dad, next dad in a gruff voice "Dennis get in here I have called you once. "Dennis scampered in, in a serious mood we got into the house and Dennis said "I am playing with my friends. "Dad looked serious at Den and said "Not anymore your not, I want you in at once." I spoke "Can I go out later as the boys are waiting for me? It's early." Dad replies "No you won't be out anymore tonight and that's final." I looked at mum she shrugged her shoulders and looked at me as if to say don't ask me I don't know what's happening. As I walked in, I saw this man again sitting on the arm chair with a large orange book opened up, we had to all sit down and this man started talking. His name was Jim Lewis; he spoke "Hello to you all, I have arranged with your father to sit down and study the bible with you all and to give you some insight into the word of our god whose name is Jehovah and by learning to understand the word of god then we can gain everlasting life and, in this book, it tells us how. The book is called Paradise Lost to Paradise regained." Den asked "What's that he's got? He is talking like the man on the news ha, ha, ha. "Dad growls at Den "Quiet Dennis, you must be quiet while Jim is talking ok? "Jim then said "Oh don't worry ray, he will get used to me talking. Does anyone know much about the bible? "No one answered and he continued "Well as you probably know the bible is the word of god or as he is known Jehovah and for the next few weeks, we shall learn to understand what his word is all about and we shall all get involved in the meeting we are holding here. But first I will ask you all to bow your heads and we shall pray." Well everyone bowed their heads except Dennis who just sat there and was wondering what the heck was going on, I looked at Den and he looked at me and let out a little laugh and nearly dropped me in it. I was confused, I was wondering what it was all about and why were we doing this at all? Den and I had been down to the Salvation Army Hall a few times to listen to the stories of the bible but that was only for half an hour and back out to play afterwards. This was going to last for one and a half hours and my friends were going to go off on their own and I was staying in because it was going to be dark by the time he had finished and Den was not the kind of boy to sit still for long, I was waiting for something to kick off with Den any minute and it wasn't long. Den not paying attention looking out of the window with his back to Jim and dad said "Excuse me Jim, Dennis turn around and pay attention." Den turned and looked at dad and Jim and smiled and after a few minutes turned back to look out of the window, so dad stopped Jim again feeling awkward "Excuse me a minute Jim" Dad grabbed Den by the arm and put him on another seat so as he could not see out of the window and said to Jim "Sorry about that, he is mentally retarded and has a short attention span but he will learn." Den looked serious and mum threw dad a nasty look. I was wondering what was going on, how was we to act at that young age. Well it was a great relief when he finished after an hour but it seemed like about 3 hours to us boys and all we had to look forward to was bed after he had finished. Well it was only one night, or was it? And yes, it was going to take over our lives and we had no choice. Dad had got religion almost immediately and life changed for us all it turned from 1 hour on Wednesday to another half an hour every evening before bed when we had to read the text book for that date like a book with chapters applying every date of that year then Thursday we went to meetings that lasted 2 hours Sunday for another 2 hours and then a Tuesday for another hour and fifteen minutes and then we were expected to go around the doors telling neighbours and other people about this religion and sell them the Watchtower and the awake magazines and it became totally embarrassing calling on my friend's houses, I felt humiliated. Melvyn however took to it like a duck in water and became dad's pet as he loved this new way of life.

Well even Dennis loved the meetings and liked meeting the girls in the Kingdom Hall and every Jehovah's Witness seemed to be very nice at all times. I however got very confused and was like a fish out of water, my dad had decided my life even if I didn't like it at all but I and Dennis were going to get involved and become Jehovah's witnesses whether we liked it or not we were made to listen or else. Dennis one day started talking to one of the witness's daughters who was about 8 years old and to my amazement dad told him to stand by my dad and not to move as if dad was worried that Dennis would maybe jump on her or something, so things have not changed all that much as far as Den was concerned.

Then there were assembly meetings every so many months in places such as Barry memorial hall or Cardiff Maindy stadium when all the many brothers and sisters of the Jehovah's witnesses from all of South Wales would collect together for 3 and a half days of meetings and talks etc. I barely found time for school let alone go out to play with my friends these days and to top that off dad kept me and Dennis hard at looking after his rabbits and chickens and the planting and weeding of his garden and many times going down the woods to collect bracken and dry it out for rabbits bedding and many more things. Dennis and I were losing our childhood and were forgetting to be kids I even took up smoking at the age of 9 just to rebel.

It was my birthday on April 3rd and mum was going to get my birthday card and present and talked to dad she said "I am off to Bridgend to get something for Danny's birthday and a birthday card tomorrow, so do you want anything from Bridgend? Dad replies snappily "There will not be any more birthdays in this house it is not the done thing in our religion anymore, it is forbidden." Mum looking shocked and stunned says to dad "What do you mean? That is ridiculous and stupid, you are taking this Jehovah's Witness thing too far now." Dad red in the face says "I am sorry Eileen but that is my final word on the matter, there will be no more birthdays celebrated in this house and while on the subject Xmas is a pagan celebration and we do not anymore celebrate Xmas anymore ok?" Mum went into a rage with my dad and said "Well Ray you are going too far now and I will get a present for Dan If I want to and you and the bloody Jehovah's witnesses can go to hell as far as I am concerned, I will live my life as a free person and if I want to get my son a present then I will." Dad says in reply "Please don't make this an issue I am the head of this family and if you go against my word there will be hell to pay, I mean it Eileen" Mum said "You are like a madman with this religion, it's taken over your life but you will not take my children's childhood away as they will one day turn against you and you know it so cut it out before it destroys this family ray." Dad just walked away and mum started crying and looked heartbroken.

Well it was the day of my birthday and I got out of bed excited but there was a solemn silence at the breakfast table until mum spoke seeing I was expectant. Mum says In a sad voice "Happy birthday my boy sorry I was forbidden to get you a card or present by your so called Dad, but you can ask him why when he comes home from work but here's half a crown for you to spend on anything you like from the tuck shop or anything else, but don't tell your dad I gave it to you or it will cause a huge argument with us all ok?" Looking at mum I could see she was very upset by all of this and I said sadly "Ok mum I won't say anything but I hate this way of life dads putting us through it's like being slaves and I hate it. We used to be such a happy family until that Jim Lewis turned up, remember?" Mum looking tearful says "I know son but never mind we will have a lovely time behind your dad's back." I smiled and went off to school.

Life got very boring and Den was affected by this the most as he had the mental problems along with now having to change his life to being made to do things he never understood or want to follow, every time he heard Jim arrive or he was about to be called in or had to get ready for meetings he would conveniently disappear. Dad was not having any of this and Den was corrected by making him stay in his room or stand in the corner many times and was also spanked with the slipper and this also applied to myself too many times and this was a huge shock to me and Den as dad had never put his hand on us until he came a Jehovah's witness as they approved of punishment to correct children in a big way and so I had a red bum for the next 9 years and made my and Dens life a total misery too much punishment for the least little thing and we both became very afraid of dad, is this normal? We were like child slaves and was kept from having any fun at all.

Den and I one day decided to go off the usual track in Glannant woods to get some bracken and found a tree swing and we decided to play with this swing and forgot all about the bracken and time just flew and we had been on this swing for nearly 3 hours and was having a fabulous time of it until dad turned up in a rage he said "what the hell are you 2 up to? I was expecting you home an hour ago with the ferns for me to put them out to dry out for the rabbits and here you are both having fun on a swing and no ferns, so get home and find my slipper I will be behind you now." Den and I tried to explain we had forgot and it was no use I could see the steam coming from dad's ears and we were in trouble for such a simple thing. We got home and in turn bent over the bed and slippered about 4 times and hard so hard it took our breath away and this was just too much for small lads like us, we just wanted to be like normal lads our age and have some fun. This was affecting mum badly and we could hear her having a go at dad saying ."you like it don't you? Hitting them little lads nearly every day they have punishment it's ridiculous Ray this bloody religion is going too far now it's overkill and must stop." Dad looked at mum seriously and said "Better now than when they are older and turn to criminals, they must be punished if they do wrong and that's that." Mum replies "You must be kidding they are not that bad just kids having some fun, didn't you have fun when you were a kid? And did it hurt you?" Dad turned his head a way and says "There must be discipline in this house and I never used to hang around the streets I was always in the woods learning not playing football with a load of idiots we done sensible things when I was a kid." Mum tutting says "Well there we are then you were poor in them days and I know it is not much better these days but you must let these boys have their childhood, they seem to be working like a coalminer and no fun, c'mon Ray let them have a childhood." Then I could hear the back door close as he went to settle his precious rabbits down and we could hear mum crying. Well at least we knew our future as dad dictated it for us and I felt Den was very troubled with this at all times and was not enjoying life at all now and could not understand why it has changed. A few days later the summer holidays started 6 weeks off school time to party, well maybe for the rest of the villager children but not for Dennis and me and so it continued Dennis and me like child slaves and very little time for playing and Den was about to go to a new place in Aberkenfig for retarded children to try and teach them any skills they could do and Den was excited about this and he was ready for September to get started and this was a new idea sent from the government for lads and girls like den, this place was a brand new building built alongside the river and very nice and all the people like Den from all the valleys will be sent there to learn. I and my parents were also excited about this for Den's sake and hoped the future was going to look up for Den at last, he needed a break.

Anyway, the summer was beautiful and even we worked hard dad was in work most of the time and he left us chore's and we made sure we did it before he got home or else. This made me and Den a lot closer even when we were fighting and we were both getting bigger and a force to reckon with and we got more respect from the other kids from our village.

Well Den started his new adventure in the new place in Aberkenfig and was very happy as he met new girls just like him and was acting like a grown up now or at least he thought like that. He was always talking about his time there and how he was in charge of the mini bus he travelled in every day and seemed a lot happier except when he had to come home and then get changed to help me care for the rabbits and gardens then 2 hours change again to go to meetings in the Kingdom hall etc. this got a bit monotonous and felt unfair at all times and lots of bad feelings were behind me and Dennis about all of this.

Well it hit rock bottom one day when den said to dad "I am not feeling well and can't go with you to the meeting tonight" dad's face said it all and he said to Den "so what's the matter with you then Dennis?" den said with serious face "oh I got a bad stomach and feel sick all the time" dad replies "well you was fine a few moments ago when you was feeding the rabbits and laughing with Danny" Den scratched his head and ear nervously and said "well I am not joking it is bad now" Dad shook his heads and said "I think that you are telling me lies aren't you?" Den looked nasty at him and said "no I am not "Dad said "you go and get ready for the meeting there's a good boy." Just then Den started to bite his hands and getting upset in his way as always and growled "look I am not well and want to stay home with mam" but Dad dismissed this and told Den to go and get ready now. Mum spoke up and with serious face says "look Ray he is telling you he is ill and does not feel well enough to go to the meeting so leave him here with me for goodness sake, what's the matter with you." Dad turned on mum and snarled "Eileen he might pull the wool over your eyes but I am not stupid." Mum shouts at dad "don't be so almighty Ray and give him the benefit of the doubt because you don't know if he is telling the truth or not." Dad started fuming and shouted up to Den "I will be up there now Dennis and you had better be getting ready or else." Mum smirked and said "you're an idiot and like a mad man and turning your children against you, you know." Dad in a temper went right up to mum's face and snarled again "he is making it all up and he will let you believe he is ill because he knows you will believe him, so let me sort this out ok? And keep your nose out because that is what he wants is for you to speak up for him, he is not all that daft." Mum just sat down and looked devastated and just put her head in her hands and sobbed. I felt so sorry for her and this was becoming the norm in this family just bickering and arguing all the time no more family loving life was to be had in the Duckfield family and poor Den just could not understand all of this and I felt his temper was not doing him any good and not even Dad seemed well for all this bad temper in the household. Well after a lot of arguing with Dennis he was forced to go to the meeting but he did not speak to Dad all that evening and looked so sad.

Well Den was having a great time with his new made friends in the centre at Aberkenfig and was acting more grown up lately and seemed to smile more while he was there. Then one day dad turned up at the centre to have a word with the manager running the centre to see how den was doing there.

He spoke to the man who run the centre "Oh hello my name is Ray Duckfield and you have my son Dennis in this centre and I was wondering how he is doing?" The head replies "yes I know Dennis he is a lovely lad and a credit to your family and yes he is settling in well here and gets on with all the other students here." Dad then says "I am enquiring about any biblical lessons etc. he is having, so can you fill me in on this please?" The head looking uneasy says "Well there are no bible studies here but sometimes we go along to the church at Christmas and Easter but other than that and of course morning assembly nothing. Why do you ask?" Dad with serious face replies "Well I must ask you to excuse him as from today on from any assembly meetings and no more church visits please as I am a Jehovah's Witness and we forbid any involvement with other religions." The head looking shocked says "Oh I see, well I will make arrangements to have him sit in his class room and get a member of staff to watch him and the same will happen when we go to Christmas mass etc. no problem Mr Duckfield even though I find this a little trivial as we all worship one god don't, we?" Dad replies "Do we? I feel we choose to do it in different ways and not perfectly as I see it as Jesus was not born on December 25 it is just an excuse for a lot of nonsense, I am afraid and I hope you will respect my wishes please." "Well yes I have no problem with that I must respect your wishes." Dad stands up and says "Thank you sir and Gooday to you "Then dad left for home.

Den seen dad that day and was panicking as to why he was there and it went through his mind, I wonder why he is here and if he is trying to get me out of here so I can take care of his rabbits and do lots of work in the house and just keep on going to meetings forever. Poor Den was surely troubled with this and was acting funny for a long time especially when he was left out of morning assembly and no more trips to church etc. well this took it's toll on him for a long time, but one day den came home from his work and was not happy at all and was very quiet this particular day and when dad came in he said to dad " the man in work said you stopped me going into assembly with my friends and no more chapel they said and you told them to stop me." Dad turned to him and replied "Yes I did as you are a Jehovah's Witness and we don't worship with any other religions ever so I told your leader there not to send you to them anymore, is that ok?" Den went red in the face and said in a nasty mood "well they are my friends and it's none of your business to tell them this I am big now "dad snapped "well your not the one to decide this, I am so that's it no more." Den started to bite his fist and snarled at dad "they are my friends and I am going with them as they all laughed at me staying in my work room so mind your own business ok?" Dad now was getting annoyed with him and replied "you will do as your told do you understand mister?" Still nasty den says "you keep out of my works and leave me alone or I will tell someone about your nastiness ok? I will go with my friends." Dad now not happy said to him "right mister up those stairs until you can behave yourself ok, go on, and stay there until I say " den now ranting and biting his fist says " you go away and leave me alone now or else I will" before he could say any more dad grabs him and says "right come on up the stairs now or the next thing will be the slipper" dad drags him to the door leading up the stairs and den was growling and screaming "get off, get off, or I will sort you out and tell the police about you, you are cruel you are I will sort you out mind" dad shouts "now get up them stairs before I sort you out and no out for you tonight, go on " Den stormed out and up the stairs mumbling all the way up in between tears. Dad stormed back in the room and mum was almost crying and about to say something to dad when he said "don't you bloody start now because I am fed up with interference from you too, I mean it Eileen, Danny get up and feed them rabbits now." I rushed up the stairs to change quickly and up their Den was crying and he stopped and said to me "he is mad that man, I will sort him out one day. You tell him for me that I want to be with my friends ok?" Danny replied "allright but he will not listen to me Den but don't worry about it just ignore it ok?" Den "he is horrible and I can't wait for him to go to work" I rushed down and went out to feed the rabbits so I could go out to play football outside in Ducko park just in front of the house but Den stayed in his room and you could see him watching us playing football from his bedroom window and he was actually smiling by now.

Well Den never went back to assembly or on outings to the chapel or church ever again with his workmates and got used to another unjust action by Dad. It was some months later when we had the biggest snow in the valleys for a long time and this was like gold to Dennis as he loved snow and was the night before watching the weather forecast on the television and rubbing his hands full of smiles and very excited and many actions was made by him making gestures as to how the snow will come down and this was something to witness from a man who was supposed to be stupid as most people seen him but not Den, I sometimes think he knew exactly what he was doing and the idiots were all the rest of us. Well the next day the snow came but Dennis never slept a wink that night he was back and forth the bedroom window watching for it to start and yes you guessed it it was about 5am in the morning, I was woken up by him laughing and very excited rubbing his hands and a massive smile was on his face and he was chatting away to me so very happy to see snow and stood in the window all morning and I fell back to sleep.

Well I finally woke up and I could hear dad down stairs moaning about not being able to get to work and Dennis was laughing his head off at the window and he said to me "Dan look at all this snow out here, no more road it is all covered and white and it is still snowing heavy, come and see" I got up and it was freezing in the room and Den must have been freezing cold but he did not care at all the snow was more important, so I had a look outside and I was amazed to see nothing really as everything looked the same tons of snow everywhere and dads motor bike and sidecar was under the snow and hardly recognisable and it was still snowing like hell and no sign of stopping and Den was almost dancing on the spot with all his excitement and saying "oh yes, oh yes, I am stuck in the house with all the snow out there and I want more to come all day ha, ha, ha, what do you think Dan?" I sat back in my bed pulled the clothes over me and smiled and said "God Den you are all excited, aren't you? You would have thought you had never seen snow before ha, ha, ha; you really are excited, aren't you? Do you fancy going out in it later and have a snow ball fight" Den laughed and replied "ha, ha, ha, no thanks they can hurt and I might slip on my bum ha, ha, you go and throw snow balls at dad ha, ha, and Mel ha, ha, I am staying in the house and watch from the window. Look at all that snow coming down from the sky ha, ha." Den loved it and dad tried to get to work by walking but failed and came home frozen and decided to wait for the snow to stop and try and clear around his motor bike and the paths around the house, but was it going to stop as it didn't seem as if it was and that pleased Den very much.

Well a little later it stopped and the ground was about 3-foot-deep and drifted in some places a lot deeper and then Dad shouts "right Danny and Dennis let's get our wellies and coats on and clear this snow around the house and over my bike." Dennis face was a picture as he looked at dad as if to say surely you don't mean me, I am not doing that, but dad told him he had to and so Danny, Dennis and dad got on with it and it was very cold on the hands and all the time Dennis was mumbling to himself and dad and Danny was laughing at him until even Den was smiling.

Well although it was so cold the 3 of them were having some fun clearing this snow and this was unusual and when they were clearing from around the motor bike Danny and Den started to pile the snow up and make a snowman and it became fun and den with all his excitement says "how do we make his head?" Danny smiled and says "I don't know." Hearing this dad chirped up "come with me I will show you." Dad and the boys went to the top of the hill on Ducko park and dad says "right lads let's make a small round ball and then I will show you what to do." The lads did as dad says with frozen hands and runny noses and dad said "now roll it down the hill slowly and it will pick up snow as we do it and get bigger and bigger. "so this they did and lo and behold it worked until they got to the body of the snowman and then Danny and Dennis struggled to get it up onto the shoulders of the body of the snowman and they were laughing their heads off and Dennis says "oh dear dad it is too heavy and Danny is too weak to lift it can you help us?" and as dad went to bend down he slipped and fell in the snow and Dennis and Danny burst out laughing and so did dad and they were slapping their hands to get them warm at the same time, Den in between laughs says "that was funny falling in the snow and now you are all covered in snow and mam is laughing by the window look, ha, ha, I am freezing and can't feel my fingers" Danny says "well blow in them like me and they will thaw out and we can pick dad up and put the head on the snowman ha, ha, ha,ha." And then Dad started laughing so much he could not get up to his feet and that made them laugh even more and when dad tried to get up, he slipped down again and that made them laugh even more and mam was wiping the tears of laughter off her cheek. Well they finished off the snowman and all of a sudden a snowball hit dad on the back of the head and he turned and some kids across the road was laughing and dad says "right Danny and den get some snowballs and get them kids over there. "And all of a sudden there were snowballs flying everywhere and lots of laughter filled the air until it got so cold, they all stopped and went in to the warm.

In the house and lots of laughter continued and they all cuddled up to the coal fire until they were all very warm and mum made some cups of Oxo with a little pepper in them to warm up their insides and she said "there we go it is much warmer in here isn't it? And I will make a bit of cowl for dinner a good stew to warm us all up tonight." Dad replies "yes that is a good idea Eileen and after that we will feed the rabbits and chickens early and stay in the warm tonight is it?" They all agreed and Dennis says "I wonder if our snowman will be there in the morning or will those kids smash it up? I loved making that snowman it was fun and no busses today or anything else and I wonder if we will have more snow tonight, I hope so I love the snow ha, ha."

Mum seemed to have a lovely smile on her face seeing us all enjoy ourselves for a change and it felt good but how long will this last? Probably until the snow melts. They fed the animals and watched some telly and had a lot of fun that night and Dennis was still in the window most of the night watching the snow he loved the snow and he seemed to have a rare glow in them winters that was so lovely to see.

Well the snow lasted all week although 3 miles down the valley the roads were clear and life was back to normal but we were very high up and it was if it was the end of the world until the snow ploughs got through and yes Den was out watching these huge lorries doing their work and his face said it all lots of smiles for all the drivers but sadness when the snow was all gone.

CHAPTER 4

Bettws the top of the world

Bettws, if you mentioned this place to outsiders from the village, they would screw up their faces and mock the village and those who lived there, but they did not know the beauty of the place as we who lived there. What is there not to like? It was so very high and the weather would sort the men out from the boys and there was another mountain above that and if you went up there and looked down on Bettws village it looked like a cocoon or a Catherine wheel it all looked so lovely as pictured on the rear cover of this book and comfortable in design and very stunningly beautiful in the summer months and even when it was covered in snow. Never mind which way you went to get out of Bettws you hit countryside and lots of it this village was totally surrounded by wild life and natural beauty, Den and I would live the life in the woods and streams and wildlife for all our childhood with no worries about anyone or anything we had Glannant woods lots of trees with hazel nuts growing everywhere blackberries by the ton groundnuts, crab apples, wild Rhubarb, strawberries, wild fish in the streams and rivers surrounding the village and much, much more and on the top of the mountains and all around it we used to pick carrier bag after carrier bag of mushrooms end of every summer so what is there not to love about this village? I feel most of the people who lived outside Bettws were jealous of our good fortune at living in some lovely surroundings. Everybody knew everybody and all looked out for each other a lovely place to bring up your children and places around us such as Pandy, the starling woods, Glannant woods, Molgelau Mountain, Shwt pond, the forestry and much, much more, never a dull time in this village. Neighbours such as the Barnet's Williams, the Evans, Webster's, the Popes, Roberts, the Griffiths, Owens, Kendall's, the Chizwells, the Martinsons, Hodges, Powlucks, Pallisters, Roses, Amos, Parkins, Larcombs, Pits, the Jones, Andrews, Richards, Pothecaries and on and on wonderful people and you could not wish for nicer people.

In the winter however Bettws was like the north pole and houses used to Freeze up all water in the houses would freeze solid and many times the water pipes would burst but it made us kids harden up and became used to it being so cold we would walk around as if it was nothing and any snow or ice and we were stranded many times. The Colliers busses would not get through to get the miners to work. Mind you if we got stranded we all had lots of fun and I remember myself Wyndham and Dennis would walk down to Brynmenyn 3 miles away on top of the drifting snow and pick up many black bags of bread for many people especially the old aged to eat and keep them happy and lots of the time we thought it was an adventure and felt great when it was all over and Den was like a horse with all of his strength that used to amaze me he could hold my arms and I could not move a muscle he was so powerful. Den with his bent nose and sloping mouth looked so loving when he was very cold and smile that could melt anyone's heart at any time and he was a gentle man at all times although he was taunted many times in his life and many times went out of everyone's way to avoid any tension.

Bettws was a place that Den loved to live in he could see the sea in Porthcawl some 10 miles away from his bedroom and in the night you could see the lighthouse flashing there every night it was amazing how far you could see from Bettws so it must have been so high and if I rode my bike to Bridgend it was so easy as it was downhill all the way but coming back to Bettws was like a Mr Universe trial totally murder but so beautiful however way you left the village and the people of Bettws were so proud of our village and surrounding areas.

Well the winter went on for at least 2 more months and it was now April and yes Dennis was still watching out for snow but still loved going to his workshop in Aberkenfig and meet up with people just like him then one day we had a tragedy in our family my grandmother in the Wyndham valley died suddenly and Den and I were very upset on hearing this sad news so much that we both had huge problems in school and Den had a problem with his feelings as he and nan were so close because with all the trouble Den had she stood up for him so many times and I recall how he Reacted when Dad came in one afternoon after we all got back from school and den's workshop he sat us down and said " Allright lads? I am sorry to tell you both that Nan in Ogmore has died today" I started to cry immediately but Den sat there as if he was in a trance which worried me and Dad. Den then started to shake and say things in a sullen mood "who? Nan is not dead I saw her last Friday, I expect she is just sleeping so don't say silly things dad" Dad replied "no Den she has died and you and I will never see her again, are you ok with that? As Grampi is even though he is so sad about it all." Den saw me crying so bad he then started crying severely and said in a sorryful voice "no she is not don't say that I need her to look after me she promised I could stay up with her next month when I am on holiday, we can't do anything without nan can we?" then he sobbed wildly and mum came into the room and was also crying it was so sad and this has hit us all so badly but Dennis was beside himself with grief and we all got a bit worried when he went outside and shut the door. Dad followed him out and Den was pulling hard on a downpipe from the roof and screaming "No, no, no, this is not true she can't leave me alone with you, I don't want her to go away I need her dad, stop her please, and go on." Dad put his arms around Dennis and said "c'mon Den I know it's awful but we must be strong for her and Grampi, and mum and I are worried about you so let's stop and think about nan and we can say goodbye in a few days ok?" Den was beside himself and was crying so badly now and started to bite his hand and tears were running down his face and he was stamping his feet on the ground then he screamed out loud "no Nanna, no, I need to come and stay with you don't go away we must have fun and go and put flowers on Queenies grave like we always do, I will get ready to pick flowers with you and I will be a good boy for you" Dad grabbed Den to stop him doing harm to himself and squeezed him and said "c'mon boy its ok, its ok, I know c'mon Den it's going to be allright you will see" Den put his head on dad's shoulder and cried and cried for ages.

In the house and mum and Danny were talking whilst in tears and she said "allright Dan I am so sorry but nan was old and we must remember all the good times we all had together do you remember? I do she was a wonderful woman and I will miss her badly, but now I need you to do me a favour, I need you and Dennis to go down to tell Melvyn later down his girlfriend's Kathleen down her mother's in Sarn can you do that and take Dennis with you to cheer him up will you? he loves to go on the bus and it will cheer him up, can you do that for me?" Danny rubs his eyes and says "yes ok, I can do that I will go and get ready will you get Dennis in and tell him to get ready too." Mum rubs her eyes and says "yes I will sort him out now and let's remember Nan as she was ok?" Danny nods his head in agreement and goes off to get ready.

Mum goes out to tell Dennis what was happening and found him still sobbing a little with dad with tears in his eyes also she then said "ok you pair? I have told Danny what is happening and Den if you get washed and changed you can go on the bus with Danny to let Melvyn know ok? Den's eyes lit up and he said "what now? Ok I will get ready "and off he trotted, dad looked devastated and sad and him and mum just went in and sat there looking totally dejected for the rest of the week.

Danny and Dennis went down to Sarn to tell Melvyn.

On the bus and Dennis is usually excited and watches the driver like a hawk but this time he was just not interested at all and was silent and then Danny spoke to him "ok Den? You are very quiet, aren't you?" Den scratches his head and replies "I hope Nan is ok, and dad tells lies." "Den don't say that, Nan has died but it's not very nice I know but she was very old and we must think nice things about her or she would be sad if she seen you was sad and remember she used to tease you and make you laugh ha, ha, remember?" Den starts to smile thinking about nan teasing him and sticking out her teeth and making faces and he laughs and says "Nan used to be silly and even mammy used to laugh at her and she used to tell grandad off remember and he used to make faces behind her back." Dan "Yes wasn't that funny and we should be smiling every time we think of Nan as she was so funny, so let's not be so sad ok?" Den replies "Mel will be sad when we tell him I bet, he loved nanny also I bet he will be crying." "yes, I think you are right den but we must be happy for nan "The bus arrived at the white bridge in Tondu and they got off it and walked down the long black path to where Mel was and as they walked in Mel met them and said "Allright boys? So where are you off then?" Danny with stern face replies "Dad sent us to see you and tell you that Nan in Ogmore died earlier." There was a deadly silence and Mel's face hardened and he put his hands over his eyes and started to cry. After a few minutes and a calming cuddle from his girlfriend Kathleen Mel says "oh my goodness no, no, I don't believe it, so when did this happen?" Dan replies as den starts to cry again "sometime this morning but dad never told us until we got home from school as dad came home early from work when he was told." Mel puts his arms around Dennis and comforted him and says "Ok Den? I know, I know she was so special to you, wasn't she? But we all loved her, didn't we? How is dad? Upset I bet." Danny says "not really he has had time to get over it I think but mam is very upset." Mel says "oh dear, that lovely woman I will miss her so much, I really will it will be a different life now without her, oh dear I don't believe it she was such a fit woman she really was." Kathleen comforts him and says "I never met her but heard such wonderful things about her, I am so sorry boys, fancy a cup of tea?" all said yes and off she goes then they all got into a group cuddle. Mel says "Oh dear, it's a funny old life isn't it? Nan was a hard-working woman especially during the war years a real true Welsh woman and as hard as nails, never mind lads we must smile and think how much fun she was, what do you think?" Den still crying murmurs "I don't want Nanny to go she loves me and wants to take care of me like she always has she will be back to normal soon." Mel replies "no Den we will not see her for a long time until she is resurrected back onto this earth sometime in the future." Den smiles and looked surer now and then in come the tea and things got back to a more normal setting.

Well Nan's funeral went off and life got back to normal and Den was enjoying himself in his workshop in Aberkenfig and dad kept out of Den's way at the centre and I felt Den was happier than he has been for a long time. Den seemed so confused most of his young life and could never grasp many things in his life but I helped him as much as I could and along with Mel made him understand many things. He came home one day and declared he has got a girlfriend and I remember it because it caused such a fuss with dad. Den arrived home off his mini bus and said to mum "Hey mum I got a girlfriend and she is very pretty and she says she loves me the best out of the whole school." Den had a huge smile on his face until dad said "you had better not be messing with any girls down their mister or I will be going down there to see your head master." Den's face turned serious and he said "Why? We are not hurting anyone so stay away from my school please because she is my girlfriend." Dad was just about to have a go at Dennis when mum says "for goodness sake Ray he is only having a nice friendship with the girl, they are never on their own to do anything you are thinking about so leave the boy alone, he has got enough to put up with the way he is so don't make a huge fuss about nothing." Dad's face went stern and he just lost it when hearing this and he stated "We must be careful with these things he is mentally retarded and I don't want mothers and fathers knocking my door complaining about his not treating her right, so Den I don't want you messing with this girl just say hello and be friends no touching her or kissing her ok?" mum "For goodness sakes Ray have faith in him he is harmless and your son have some thought how he feels and I can't see him raping her he has not got the mind to think of something like that for Christ sake." Dad now fuming says "Do you have to take the lords name in vein and he will do as he is told and that is the end of it, are you listening Dennis?" Den scratches his ear and mumbles something that no one could understand and dad jumps up and shouts "I beg your pardon? What did you say then?" Den says in a temper whilst biting his fist "I am not speaking to you she is my girlfriend not a friend of yours she is with me ok? I am going to be with her and I will tell grandad and he will tell granny about you, you are cruel to me all the time, isn't he mam?" mum agrees and this made dad worse and he said "right I will stop you going to that centre, you can stay home here and do chore's every day instead "Den bites his fist and storms out of the room and Mum says to Dad "There we are he will come to hate you later in his life and so will the rest of them as you are like bloody Hitler, these boys have got no life and are losing their childhood because of your bloody religion." Dad was now fuming and stormed out of the house to do some work on his motorbike and sidecar.

It was the next day and Den was all excited to go to the centre to see his girlfriend and was like a little boy with all of this happening and as brothers we all noticed this and was teasing him at all times about her and he never got nasty at all he seemed to enjoy this until Xmas came along and he brought a note home from the centre saying this is to let you know that the xmas party will be at the centre on the 12th December and the bus will be coming back on the home run 1 hour later than normal. Please give me any reasons for any food your son\daughter cannot eat etc. Mum was given the note and decided not to tell dad and just let it happen and plead ignorance about it.

Well the day came and Dennis was all excited and was told by mum not to say anything about it to dad or his brother's and Den smiled when told this and went along with this. Off he went almost dropping Mum in it several times and mum had a terrible time keeping it from dad because of the way den was acting in front of everyone but he was in the centre having his first xmas party with his friends and girlfriend and there was a disco for them and Den loved music and was having so much fun he said to his girlfriend Mandy "Can you dance Mandy? I can let's try it." She was looking embarrassed but went out to dance with Den and they were chatting away with lots of difficulty as they were in a world of their own. Mandy said "Oh Dennis you are a good dancer, what do you think of me dancing then?" Den with huge smile on his face says "You are good and we can have a smooch later if you like." Mandy "What is a smooch ha, ha, ha," Den replies now laughing loudly "It's like a hug you know, I put my arm around you and you put your arm around me and we must whisper to each other ok?" Mandy looking confused says "Oh I don't know you will have to show me later."   "Ok I will show you if I can remember because I have only seen it in my aunties party?" They danced a lot and enjoyed themselves and then came up a smooch song and it was so funny Den showing Mandy how to do it Den said "That's it put your cheek on my cheek." This Mandy did and they looked as if they were stuck together by their cheeks and they kept on crashing into other dancers but love was in the air and they were later seen holding hands in a corner under the table. Mandy and Den knew how they both felt about each other even if other people did not understand them and this was a massive boost for Den's ego and much, much more, he was growing up weather dad liked it or not and he was a responsible person he knew right from wrong but was never given any credit for it. Even though I was some 6 years younger than him I saw him starting to grow up even if it was many years below his actual age.

Well Den came home from his Xmas party and was so excited and yes you guessed it he could not keep it to himself and dad became suspicious and said to him "Well den you are excited, aren't you? So, what have you been up to?" Den smiling and scratching his ear says "Nothing I have had a real nice time today and danced with my girlfriend

, and had a smooch with the disco in the centre." Dad seen red and says to him "Why have you had a disco in your centre then?" Den smirking says "Because it's Xmas and father Xmas was there and gave us all sweets and pencils, and we had a dance in the main hall after Xmas dinner." By now dad was seeing red and fuming and he looked at mum and said "did you know about this Eileen?" Mum shrugged her shoulders and replied "No I didn't as a matter of fact" dad did not believe her and said to Dennis "Why did you not tell me about this? and there is no such thing as father xmas." Dennis till smiling says "I know it was the boss Mr Phillips dressed up as father xmas I could tell." Dad "Well you should not have gone to that party and I will be telling the centre what I think of it "Dad then told Dennis to empty his pockets and Den resisted but dad found a party hat and some pencils. In xmas wrapping paper and took them off Dennis and threw them into the fire and den screamed at dad "no they are mine not yours." and tried to retrieve them from the fire, but the heat was too much and he failed and started crying out loud "one of those was from Mandy my girlfriend and you are horrible and I will tell Mr. Phillips about you." Dad replied looking at mum at the same time "That will teach you to do things behind my back as Jesus was not born in December and we do not celebrate xmas and that's that." Mum almost in tears says "You and your bloody religion is tearing this family apart and that poor boy does not understand any of this so what point are you making? He is going to hate you the way you are acting." Dad with smug look "I don't care as long as he stays away from the wrong side of our god "Den storms off to his bedroom and we all stayed silent listening to mum and dad arguing yet again about religion and the demands dad wanted at all times. All of a sudden dad picked on Danny and said "And what about you what are they doing in your school? and have you joined in?" Danny replied "I don't get involved in anything in my school not even in morning assembly, honest." Dad "I hope not and if I find you are telling me lies look out." Dad stormed off and mum was reeling in her seat and as soon as he leaves, she says "he has become a maniac over that bloody religion and it is worrying me." At that mum put her head in her hands and started crying and that made me feel so sad and so I tried to comfort her "it's ok mum, it's not your fault please don't cry I don't like to see you crying, c'mon mum fancy a game of cards with me?" Mum wipes her eyes with her hand and says with a little smile "oh we had better not because that will be wrong, in your fathers eyes I can't smile without him starting a fuss, but I will be allright and don't you worry about all of this." Then mum says we should make some cake and I could help her and clean the mixing bowl out when she has finished.

Well xmas was almost upon us and den was like a wild man after what had happened and one morning before he got on the mini bus for work said to mum "Mandy has gone off with my friend Jeff in the centre because I did not give her a xmas present and that's dad's fault, I hate him." Den then started crying and mum felt bad for him and said "Oh Dennis, I am so sorry but it may be for the best until you are older and find yourself a nice girlfriend" Den stamps his feet and declared "She was a nice girlfriend and I want her to come back to me she was my girlfriend first." Mum replies "Yes I know Den and I am sorry but never mind you will be allright and find yourself another girlfriend, maybe in one of the meetings. "den looking shocked says "I am not allowed to talk to any of the girls there as dad keeps on watching me all the time and stops me talking to them for long and he will not let me say much to them ever." Mum shocked says "Why do you say that? does he stop you talking to them?" Den strokes his fringe to one side says "Oh yes he is mean and I hate going to the meetings now and will not be going anymore" Mum looking sad almost started to cry but bit the tears back and said to Den "oh Den I am sorry you don't stand a chance in this cruel world and your such a harmless chap, aren't you? Your so misunderstood and they will never have the chance to get to know you. Well Den time to catch the mini bus and don't worry me and you will have some fun over the xmas period ok?" Den rubs his hands and smiled at mum and went off to his last day in the centre until the new year.

Yes, Xmas day arrived and lots of excitement in the village except for the Duckfield home where everything was just as normal as every other day. Outside was all the kids in the street playing with their new bikes, new footballs in their new football kits and many other sorts of toys and Danny and Den looking on through the window and mum almost crying with the awful sight she was seeing in front of her and by the faces on the lads it was so pitiful only little baby Lyndon was gurgling and seemed to be having fun as he was too small to realise what was going on but he would soon be old enough to understand and this would be even more hard for mum but dad kept on whistling his tunes off the records from the Jehovah's witness albums.

Den said "look at Alan jane and john Kendall's new bikes they are smart, aren't they?" Danny chirped up "Yes real nice bikes, aren't they? And look at Adrian's bike a new racing drop handle bike I bet that is fast too." This all become too much for mum and she got up and went upstairs to have a real good cry not to show the lads. Dad chirped up and said to the lads "don't forget to feed the rabbits in an hour mind I am off to see Jim in Pen-y-Bryn so make sure it is done before I get back understood?" Danny and Den said ok and dad left. Mum came down from upstairs and you could see she had been crying and the lads went up to her and gave her a cuddle and went off to feed the rabbits looking so very sad probably wondering what they had done to be so very different to all the rest of the children in the world.

Xmas was so difficult for all the family except Melvyn and Dad and the lads Dennis and Danny and Lyndon just let it all pass.

Chapter 6

Time for some sly fun.

Well Den and Danny seemed to be in a trance most of the time having to attend meetings 3 times a week doing their chores most evenings straight after school and not mixing with anyone much from school neighbours and only mixing with Jehovah's witnesses and not really in the same league as the lads totally different interests and you could see especially in Den's case he was bored and felt lost and out of his zone at all times. Den hardly spoke to the family and hid in his bedroom most of the time looking out of his window watching the world go by and slowly becoming a recluse and mum could see what all this was doing to the boys and decided to do something about it. She started to go down to her sisters in Pencoed again every Saturday and took the boys with her every time whether dad liked it or not.

It was one day in her sisters she was talking to Mabel and she said to mum "oh there is a get together for the family in 2 weeks in the legion club here as it is Gwyn and Marlene's wedding and it's a pity you are not coming Eileen it will be a good day, can't you come for the day it's your brother after all." mum looked up to the heavens and says with a cunning smile on her face "Yes I know I have been thinking about it all month and have decided to grab the lads and come to the wedding and Mel said he would pick us up in his camper van but I have mentioned it to Raymond and he has not said much and I think he will not come himself so we could have a little fun for a change with him out of the way and I could stay here if it is allright until the evening party and Melvyn has arranged a mini bus to take us all home in the evening is that allright with you Mab?" "Of course, it is Eileen and what about Ray will he agree to it?" Mum replies "He will have to, I am doing it whether he likes it or not, I am not living for him anymore and the lads will be with me and Ray can stay at home and whistle to his Jehovah's records until his lips crack, ha, ha, ha, sorry Mab I have had enough of his ways and his bloody religion and I will be at Gino's and Marleen's wedding he is my youngest brother and that is that." Mabel laughing says "Well done Eileen time you stood up to him and got back to your own family as we miss you and the family very much." Mum "I know I am fed up with it all with him and he is setting his sons against him because of his fanatic way with religion and if he keeps it up, he will be on his own I am sorry." Mabel looking serious says "Really it has got that bad has it? I am afraid I would have got rid a long time ago I can see what you have had to put up with and I think you deserve a medal and I can see in Dennis he is always looking so sad and gets very excited when he is down here seeing his cousins." Mum puts her head in her hands and starts to cry and mumbles "Oh Mabel you don't know the half of it especially this xmas just gone those lads were watching all the neighbours kids with all their new bikes and toys and they had nothing it was so sad to see and Ray didn't blink an eyelid it broke my heart I felt as if they felt they had done something wrong I just cried and cried." Mabel puts her arms around mum and looked so upset for mum and she said "Oh I don't like seeing you like this Eileen, c'mon now things can only get better and them lads will remember this when they are older and then you will see the real happy lads, I wish there was something I could do it hurts so much." Mum wipes the tears from her eyes and starts to smile at her sister and says "I am allright Mabel it is silly of me and we will enjoy ourselves some other way don't you worry." Mabel makes a cup of tea and they spend the rest of the day reminiscing over the war years and having a good laugh as the lads were outside playing with their cousins and no dad to put a stop to their fun.

Dennis and Danny were growing up together like a pair of twins and Danny was getting into fights over people making fun of Den even if the other lads were bigger than him and Danny often sported a black eye because of Dennis.

Well it was the day of Gwyn and Marlene's wedding and Dennis, Danny and Lynden were so excited but were told by mum to keep it to themselves until they had left the house. Uncle Melvyn from Sarn came up to pick them up in his Volkswagen camper van and off they went and the excitement on Den's face was a wonderful thing to see especially with his uncle Mel who often teased Den and Den loved it and was rubbing his hands together a lot showing his pleasure and he loved all his cousins and was in heaven and this put a huge smile on mums face and I think sometimes a few tears of pleasure for her children at last. They were all singing in the van on their way across Heol-Y-Cyw common as in them days it was all A roads no dual carriageways or motorways and really hardly any traffic on the roads and this made for a pleasant journey for all the both families and Den was mad about any sort of car, lorry, bus, or any type of vehicle and he would watch every move uncle Mel was doing as he drove the camper.

Aunty Marjory loved to play and tease Den and she said "Well Dennis have you been a good boy for your mum?" Den with a cunning smile replied while looking at mum says "Yes I have haven't I mum?" Mum starts to laugh and replies "Well yes and no, he has been good for me but has played hell with Ray, especially when he went to the xmas party in his place and never told his father and Ray went berserk ha, ha, ha, but then ray took his xmas present off him and threw it in the fire and it really upset the boys especially Den, didn't it mate?" Den's face turned serious and he nervously started to scratch his ear and that told everyone he was unhappy and he said "Yes he did and he is horrible and nasty and I don't like him anymore." Maj smiling says "Never did he? That's awful he might not believe in Xmas but that is going too far, never mind Den we will have a beer and some fun tonight in the party ok?" Den's face turned back to a huge smile and he starts to rub his hands together again and replies "Yes ok I can drink a few beers and I can have a dance with Debbie if you like." Den's cousin Debbie speaks up "Ok Den we will have to dance to the music I like mind." Den laughs and says "Ok I don't care I can dance very good now and Mandy my old girlfriend liked to smooch ha, ha, and it was nice." Maj looked up and said "I will be watching you Dennis no hanky panky with my girls ha, ha, ha, and uncle Mel will be watching as well so look out." Den doubled up laughing and the journey went onto the wedding.

At the church and what a wonderful wedding it was and Den was so excited by it all, huge smiles and lots of rubbing his hands together and of course he was meeting up with all his cousins he hasn't seen for ages. Well in the church and Den was not sure when it came to saying a prayer as he seemed nervous and watched mum and me and just smiled and looked down to the ground whilst everyone else closed their eyes and prayed. It seems that it is getting to Den and Danny and this was worrying for mum but Dennis managed it pretty well and after the ceremony he was not happy to have his photograph taken he had to be prompted every time and had to be made presentable every time as you could put a beautiful suit on him and he still looked scruffy and that was just how Den was and it was sometimes funny to see him play up unless he was grabbed by one of his female cousins he then would jump in and was totally ready for it.

The evening came and there was a disco that hugely made Den smile and he was in another world by now, he was sitting by his uncle's Leighton, Melvyn, Dia, Tony and his lovely aunty Mabel and was loving every minute and just then his uncle Mel said to him "Fancy a pint Den?" his face lit up and he immediately looked over to mum and she was smiling and den said "Oh yes please I love a pint of beer, I love to drink a few pints don't I mum?" Mum still smiling said "yes but don't get drunk mind." Den's face lit up yet again and he was rubbing his hands together profusely and replied "I won't I will stop if I feel too drunk ok?" mum agreed and den's uncle Mel came back with half of shandy realising he was not allowed to drink beer due to his problems but den stood very tall with his beer in his hands and he said after the first swig of beer "Oh not a bad pint is it?" and looked so grown up by now and continued "it's strong." And everyone on his table smiled at this and his uncle Leighton says "Take your time now Den I don't want to carry you out at the end of the night, are you going to have a dance with any of your cousins later?" Den slides his hands through his fringe and brushed it to one side said "oh yes I am going to dance with all of them if they want to." Uncle Mel smiled at Dennis and said "We will be watching you mind they are our daughters so behave yourself mind." Den "of course I will and I am going to ask the man playing the records to play some nice music I can dance to and even have a smooch later ha, ha, ha, I can do that as my girlfriend Mandy and I did at xmas you know, honest now." Mum smiled and said "I will watch you den so do it nice and be careful you don't fall on your bum with too much beer ok?" Den was loving all the attention and was like a child with a new toy and it took him about another hour before he got up to dance and he was up dancing for ages until he said to one of his cousins "I am having a minute now to have my pint or it will go off and it's my round ok?" Debbie who was dancing said "Dennis I hope you are not drinking with your uncles, you will be drunk drinking with that lot ha, ha, ha, and your wobbly already." Den quickly said "No I am not I can drink lots of them ha, ha, and your dad got me my last pint so it's his fault ha, ha, ha," Debbie said "Right I will tell him off now ok?" Den's face changed and he looked panicky and replied "Oh no he is ok so leave him alone or he will tell me off." Debbie seen Den was a little upset and was shocked by this and quickly said "It's allright Den I was only kidding, it's allright to have another drink as long as you don't get drunk." Den's smile reappeared and he set off to get his pint down him.

Back on the table and his uncle Ginno was there the man who's wedding it was and he said to Den "Your not drunk are you Den? I am shocked at you drinking beer." Den said smiling "I am not having many as dad will be annoyed if I do so hush don't tel him ok? I am having some real fun tonight and lots of dances ha, ha, ha." Ginno then said "Ok I will get you a beer in and no dancing with my new wife mind as I am watching you ha, ha, ha." Den looked downwards and said "Oh no she is married now I will stay with Debbie and Julie I think but I will have a couple of beers first to get in the mood." Everyone laughed at him saying this and Den sat down and sipped his pint and you could not stop him talking all night. His beer arrived and Ginno put it down on the table in front of him and Den then again looked at mum as if to get her approval which she did and went straight back into conversation with everyone. It was a real boost for Den and myself having this party after all that went wrong over Xmas and it was still in the back of our minds as to how dad would react when we got home and so we both never really settled down too much. The evening was now getting noisy with all the other people arriving and Den did not know who to talk to next but disappeared most of the night trying to talk to everyone there and he seemed to be in his element with it all and being with such a loving family made a difference to Den as he loved them all without question, they would become a huge part of his life in his remaining days. His uncle Leighton and Alma were delightful, Leighton was such a loving quiet man you could not help loving a real gentleman. Uncle Melvyn and Margery lots of fun even though Mel was a quiet man he was often teased by Marjory and a man who had his own opinions that really made a difference to my life in future years. Aunty Mabel and Tony was a lovely, lovely couple and Mabel was a woman and was the one who wore the trousers there and very quiet spoken woman and Tony loved her without question and did whatever she said and they were totally in love with each other for as long as I can remember. Uncle David or Dia as we knew him and his wife Beryl lovely people but Dia said it as it was and so did Beryl and we love them for it. Gwyn or Ginno and Marlene were the youngest of the family and he was a total character who played guitar in a band and was a bit of a comedian and was very down to earth with us at all times and his new bride Marlene was just as lovely and lots of laughs and smiles a lovely couple. Uncle Ted and Sheila another lovely couple and he was a larger than life man who lived in Australia were so much in love also but we never seen enough of them at all because they were so far away. There was another uncle living up in Buckinghamshire who we never got to know but was a lovely man by all accounts and there was mum the oldest of them all who along with my dad Raymond who were living nothing like the rest of the family and this made me sick to my stomach most of the time as she often looked so sad. I always remember how dad was, he never ever told any of us lads he loved us, he lived a serious life and never showed his feelings towards us and I felt that Dennis with all his problems needed it so much as it was such a confusing life not really understanding many things at any time, it was like living with a total stranger who dictated how your life will turn out to be and that even showed with my oldest brother Melvyn who I felt was afraid of dad and done everything by the book as dad dictated it to him. Mel was a genius at school and blew every type of grade there was to be had 11 A Levels 11 O Levels in education and would have made a million in money if he had never have become a Jehovah's Witness but he turned out to be a real gentleman and had the heart of a lion and I was proud of him ever since I was born.

Well back to my story Den had a fantastic night in Ginno's wedding party and when we got home that night it was around midnight and we went in to the house in silence as Dad had gone to bed after putting Lyndon to bed and by the smile on Den's face it was one of the best times in his life being with such a loving family as mum was.

Next day we were got up early and had to feed the rabbits and clean their cots out then have breakfast and off to the meeting in Bridgend to hear a talk for 1 hour then study the Watchtower magazine for another 1 hour, what a come down and you could see how tired den was as he fell asleep twice in the meetings and dad was not amused. Dad never said anything about the wedding and we felt relieved and kept on interrupting every time Den would try to talk about it just in case, he mentioned his beer shandy that would have caused an earthquake with dad finding out about it. Well we got away with it and on Monday dad had gone to work and we had a good laugh about it before we went to school and Den was making fun of how things went when he was drinking with his uncles and dancing along most of the night and he started to look a little grown up for once.

That evening on the Monday Den and Danny fed the rabbits and did their other chores and both of them fell asleep on the chair and it was so funny as they had enjoyed themselves so much they were exhausted and for once dad never said a word and mum looked so much happier thinking that dad was maybe mellowing a little and things went along a little easier for a few weeks until Danny was caught smoking one day by a fellow Jehovah's witness on the banking as we used to call it with a maze of paths going through it behind the houses opposite going down to the Oddfellows arms and there was Danny, Wyndham, Terry Peacock, Alan Pothecary and Victor Stanford and they were being watched from one of the bedrooms and caught red handed with a packet of 10 park drive cigarettes between them.

Dad set upon Danny as soon as he found out and Danny was told to get upstairs and bend over for the slipper and you could hear the screams as dad walloped him without mercy and mum crying with hate for what dad was doing and yes, another argument between mum and dad. Mum screamed at dad "you make me sick the way you are he is only a small boy and you hit him as if he was a grown man you cowardly bastard." Dad in a rage at what mum had said to him says "You foul mouthed woman you make me sick to my stomach and it is not good to use that language in front of the lads is it? If you were a man, I would give you a good hammering." Mum eggs him on by saying "Come on then big man, if you can hit a small child that easy it is no problem for you to hit a woman or are you afraid, I will hit you back because that is what you need someone to give you a bloody good hammering and maybe you would think again about hitting defenceless little children." Dad raged "So you think it is allright for Danny to be smoking at his age or for that matter any age and don't say I used to smoke because it was not right for me to do it either so don't say it, the lad is wrong and needs to be punished, remember when Dennis nearly died trying it and it was different then was it?" Mum told dad "Fu** off and leave my boys alone you just go too far and one day they will turn on you and I will smile when they do." Dad turns on his heels and walks out in a rage, mum comforts Danny who was crying mercilessly in her arms and Dennis was looking on and looked as white as a sheet. This was taking a toll on their lives especially Dennis who could not understand why there was so much rage and not much love coming from our own father.

Well it was back like the early days like the early 1800 and the days when they would shove children up the chimneys to clean them or so it seemed and Danny, Dennis and Lyndon kept their heads down and Mel just disappeared down his girlfriends as much as he could he was like a whippet getting his chores done and off he went to Sarn to Kathy's house out of the way.

Well another wedding came up and it was Michael Duckfield's in the Ogmore valley a nephew to my dad and this was going to be fun as we were all going even Dad and we just did not know what to expect as he was getting married in the chapel in Ogmore and then to the Non-Political club nearby and of course dad would not recognise any other religion and did not drink at all.

The day came and off we went but as we were getting ready dad sat us down and said to us "right lads when we get in the chapel to the wedding don't bow your heads when they prey just stand with eyes open and ignore what the preacher is saying and don't sing any hymns at all just stand there ok? "we all just looked at each other puzzled and agreed with him and off we went mum tut, tutting at what dad had said.

Well it went off pretty good then dad said half way through the reception "right time to go home so get ready" Den's face said it all he frowned and mum said to dad "for goodness sake Ray we have only just got here I am not leaving yet I am staying here for another hour at least, you do what you want but don't dictate to me what to do" Dad growled at this but did not want to cause a scene and left it go and they could see Dennis with a huge grin on his face and den actually had a pint of shandy in front of him and dad never said a word to him. Well eventually they left and that was that.

Chapter 5

Growing up rather quick.

Well by now Den was a lot older just turned 15 and was now not attending the centre anymore he had grown up and out of that place and defied dad much, much more by refusing to go to the centre and most meetings and dad could see he was growing into a young man although his mind was a mind of a 2 year old boy and dad was using this fact to treat him as a child which he did not like at all and rebelled as much as he could.

Den was now paying lots of attention to the opposite sex which is normal in a boy of his age but dad by now watching every move Den took and Den knew this and laughed about this with a cunning smile at most times.

Mumm was loving having Dennis around as it was company for her and he loved going up to Peggy's shop and even though he was mentally handicapped he got to know somehow if he was short changed which was amazing and Den was developing as a rather normal man of his age except in his mind.

Den was still obsessed about busses and it showed and he would pretend to be a bus and pretending to drive against the kerbstone making the noise of a bus and pulling a huge steering wheel around even making the sounds of airbrakes that made him look so silly and this annoyed Danny very much and Danny would often tell Dennis off about this and if Den seen Danny he would abandoned his bus and walk off the road and onto the pavement smiling to himself. One day dad set upon Dennis and said "Dennis look at the state of these shoes I only bought these about 2 months ago and all the sides are scuffed badly, what have you done to cause this?" Den smiling and scratching his head and ear that he usually does when he has done something wrong replies "Nothing I don't know why these are scratched, I dunno" Dad in a rage says "I know why it's you rubbing them up against the kerb while pretending to be a bus and it has got to stop I cannot afford new shoes we are struggling as it is" Den looking nervous says "I know we can take the money out of my money box ha, ha, ha," dad snaps "there's not enough to pay for the laces in your money box" Danny interrupted "I wish he would not go round the streets acting like a bus as my friends laugh and make fun of him so stop him dad please" den snarls at Danny "you shut up you I am not talking to you, you always shout at me outside and he threatens my dad." Dad says "well Dennis you will have to stop it or I will keep you in and if you continue, I will be is that clear?" Den in temper and going red in the face "it's not up to you I have got to drive my bus I am not doing any harm" Dad repeats "I don't care you had better stop it now, understand?" Den mutters under his breath and goes off to feed the rabbits and Danny followed to help him and, in the rabbits, shed Dennis puts his fist in his mouth and starts on Danny "you, you I am going to tell mum about you making fun at me when I am in my bus and she will sort you out and you leave me alone from now on ok?" Danny snarls back "if I catch you playing silly busses, I will sort you out so be careful" they then get into a massive row and dad hears this and shouts at them "right you 2 get on with your chores and in the house as soon as you can for bible studies" They both went quiet and did as they were told but that was not going to be the end of it.

A couple of days later and Danny was walking home from school and a few lads were making fun of Dennis as he was driving his pretend bus and Dennis did not take any notice and just carried on and Danny was not happy and chased after Dennis and shouted at him and den abandoned his bus and again put his fist in his mouth and started shouting at Danny "you bugger off and leave me alone or I will sort you out " Danny says "you had better be careful or I will hit you ok now get home and stop being so stupid " Den then went right up to Danny and put his head right up to Danny's face and in a wild look said out loud and spitting "I will sort you out mind " then they both started fighting and Danny got the better of Dennis and den started crying and ran off and lads around them started laughing at them both and making fun "the ducko's are mad and smelly" Danny just walked off in temper and went straight home behind Dennis and mum was waiting for Danny and was not happy. Danny walked into the house and she started on him immediately " What have you done to Dennis he has gone to his bedroom crying and said you hit him" Danny said "well he was playing his stupid bus again and some of the boys were laughing at him, he is stupid the way he is and I am not going to be made a fool of here so he had better stop it " Mum says "I thought you would have been more understanding with your brother he is mentally handicapped as you know he can't help it and he is happy in his own world and hurts nobody does he? So have some patients with him he is your brother don't forget" Danny says in reply "I don't care he is an idiot and making me look stupid and I am not having it I will sort it out if he does it again mum it's not fair why did I have to be the only lad in this village to have a brother like him" Mumm looking sad replied "I am sorry the way Dennis turned out too but he is what he is and I have been fighting everyone over him ever since he was born, will there ever be any end to this for me and him? It just goes on and on" Mum by now was close to tears and Danny felt sorry now he had said this to mum and felt for her then Dennis walked in and shouted at Danny "yes I am mentally handicapped" Danny thought then he knows he is handicapped and uses it like a normal person, so he is not that stupid after all. Mum smiled at what Dennis had said and all of a sudden he had a huge smile on his face as he looked at mum, she was the only one that has ever stood by Dennis without question since the day he had been born and you could sense the love between mum and son never mind what, Mum put a stop to the arguing that day but it was not over by no means as it seemed to happen many times until one day it took a different corner.

One day in a holiday time and Danny was walking and heard a commotion coming just down the road from their house and he went to see what it was all about and it was not what Danny wanted to see but it would change things for Dennis and Danny forever. Dennis was again playing at being a bus and Danny could see by his face he was in an angry mood and looked as if he was about to cry and behind him was a large lad a few years older than Danny and much bigger making fun at Dennis and slapping Dennis on the back along with a few lads egging the large lad on and the large lad was laughing and shouting at Dennis at the same time. Dann on seeing this clicked although this lad would probably kill Danny if he said anything but Danny was by now getting so angry at the sight he had in front of him and just charged at the bigger lad whose name was Freddie Harry and ran into him knocking him over and there was a deadly silence until he got up to his feet and Danny nervously said to him "why are you slapping my brother and shouting at him? you know he can't help it " the large lad just looked so evil at Danny and charged at Danny and hit Danny in the face and Danny got hold of him and they wrestled to the ground with blood coming out of Danny's nose and they then got up to their feet and Danny give him a few punches to the face and head butted him in the nose and he went down and never attempted to get up and go at Danny again and Danny spitting blood said " if I ever see you having a go at Dennis ever again I will not stop next time I mean it so don't ever do anything like this ever again, right den are you ok?" Dennis smirked and said to Danny "yes he was hitting me for a long time and he had better watch it from now on isn't it ha, ha, I will tell you if he does it again allright?" Danny smiled at Dennis and said "You must stop this bus business den but he will not give you any trouble again I hope as now he knows what will happen. C'mon let's go home, are you ok have you got any cuts on you?" "no, I am allright I will see you in the house "den went off rather quickly and Danny followed and all the lads around just went off with their tails between their legs. Danny still shaking was amazed at the way he reacted when he saw what was happening to Dennis and felt good for days after and Freddie Harry was wary of Danny from that day onwards.

Well Danny had a black eye and split lip and looked as if he had gone a few rounds with Mohammed Ali but he felt good about himself until dad got home and seen him and roared "what the hell have you been up to?" Danny with fear in his face thought he was about to bend over again for the slipper replied "I have been fighting with a lad down the road "Before he could say anymore dad snapped "you know I don't like fighting and I will sort this out upstairs in a minute." Then mum stormed at dad "Don't you want to know why he was fighting or do you like hitting little boys? Why don't you ask Dennis why Danny was fighting" Dennis was standing there looking nervous and said smirking "Freddie was hitting me on the back and shouting at me making fun and Danny saw it and hit him ha ,ha, ha, " Danny smiled at Dennis's explanation and said " I am his brother and I didn't like it and after he hit me I got hold of him and gave him a good bashing and he won't poke fun at Den again will he Den " Den said " no he is frightened of Danny now and most of the kids here ran off and I think they will leave me alone as I will get him to give them a hiding isn't it Dan" Dennis looked fondly at his little brother and dad spoke up "Freddie down the road? He is a big lad and a few years older than you, are you sure about this Daniel?" Danny then said " yes I know he is huge but I lost my temper when I saw what they were doing to Den and just lost it, they are not treating my brother like this anymore I am fed up with some of the kids in this village they are horrible some of them" Dad's face lit up with a huge smile and he said "well I think you were right and a chip off the old block as that is how I would have sorted it out when I was your age and a lot older, I don't like fighting anymore now I am a witness but well done Danny, well done, and you look worse than it could have been but he has got 2 brothers so be careful " Danny said "oh those 2 are no problem as now I have sorted out the oldest brother they won't try it and will also be afraid of me" Dad then said "well your growing up I can see that and hope you don't turn out like I was when I was younger but well done son it's nice for 2 brothers to stick together, let's hear no more about it, have you fed the rabbits yet?" Danny and Dennis replied together that they had and went off out after.

Danny was shocked by the events of that day and was stunned at dad's reaction and how he got away without the slipper. Danny felt a lot better after that day and most of the lads in the village showed much more respect for Danny and left Dennis alone now.

Danny's mum had a good friend in Mrs Freda Pothecary Alans mum Mrs Mr Pothecary were a lovely couple. Freda was a short woman who reminded me of the woman on the South Pacific film bloody Mary but a woman who said it as it was with a heart of gold a woman who Danny had a lot to do with for many years as Alan was a good friend to Danny, George was a very tall man who had a limp and used a walking stick and stood out where ever he went loved a laugh and loved the female of our species. Mum and Freda often went into each other's house for tea in the day when Dad was in work and often Dennis would go in with her and sit with them, well Mr Pothacary whose first name was George would have a bit of banter with Dennis and he got to like them both and George would tease him with girls like saying "have you got a girlfriend?" Den would rub his hands together and very excited say "I did have a girlfriend when I was in the centre and I like a girl living up the street " George then said " I hope you are not doing rude things with them and if not why not ha, ha, ha, " Den not knowing what he was on about just scratched his head and made a funny little face and said "oh no I am not like that " George laughing said "have a look at this in here "Den followed him into this working parlour and was shocked but excited with what happened next. George loved blue films he would watch on his cinny camera on old cellulite film on reels and this is what he would show Dennis and Dennis just stood there mouth open and smiling from ear to ear and could not keep his eyes off the girls taking off their clothes and dancing around with nothing on. George said "what do you think of that then?" Den was dumbfounded and could not speak and just shrugged his shoulders and had a huge smile on his face as if to say don't turn it off then said "where did you get this from she is nice and you know ha, ha, ha, I have never seen this before "Dennis was a dribbling wreck and could not believe his eyes and they both just sat there watching it all in silence and George was smiling. They watched the film until the end and George was smiling still and teased Dennis saying "well did you enjoy that den?" Den now scratching his ear and a massive smile on his face replied "oh yes I did have you got anymore then" and rubbed his hands together in excitement, George then said "yes but I think you have seen enough for one day ha, ha, ha, but if you like I have got a magazine you can take home with you as long as you never show your mum or dad " Den said " what's that then " George pulled out a magazine of the adult nature and said to den "hide this in your trousers and then hide it under your mattress in your bedroom and don't let dad or mum find it or they will go mad and you will be in big trouble and I will not say to them I gave it to you ok?" Den with serious face looked at the cover of the magazine and it had a nude woman on it and his face was a picture to see and he pushed it down his trousers and put his jacket on to hide it totally and George remarked "there you go it's out of sight so go straight home and hide it, I will let you out of the front door and tell your mum you have gone home in ten minutes ok? Don't show anyone ok? or I and you will be in trouble.

Den went out of the front door as fast as his legs could carry him and into the house and to his bedroom. And nothing was found by mum or dad ever but Danny did find it one day.

It was sometime now and Dennis was spending more and more time in his bedroom and this particular day Danny caught den with the magazine.

Until that day Dennis never muttered a word and no one in the house knew any different, does this mean Dennis is a normal man and not so mentally handicapped as everyone thinks? Does he have sexual urges just like any other man? He has learned by natural instinct to masturbate over an adult magazine, is this possible? Is Dennis as normal as me an you? But he has not ever even cuddled a woman let alone have any sort of sexual suggestion towards them and he has never ever put himself on to other women and been the perfect gentleman always without any question. The question must be asked is Dennis as normal as any other man or teenager of his age? has all the tendencies of normal people? Is he ever going to be a danger to other women by his attitude towards them? I have always felt Dennis was a man of love and a man with a heart of a lion and has never had a bad bone in his body and would never do anything bad as he did not know how to.

Well back to the story, Dennis seemed a little more responsible these days and hardly ever went out and stayed in his bedroom which he shared with Danny and Lynden and you would always see him with a notepad and a pen and he would pretend to write in this pad many times a day although it was just gobble-de-goo and although it was many signs he wrote were identical in rows of about forty in a row, I wonder if this meant something to him only. Den's temper settled down and he became a lovely, lovely young man and always gentle and if left alone never bothered anybody,

Dennis however was always scruffy looking you could put him in a tuxedo and he would still look scruffy, he was such an awkward looking little chap although tall and skinny with funny shape to his mouth and nose due to the plastic roof to his mouth and his speech was not getting any better and Danny still had to tell people what he was saying most of the time, but you could definitely see a change in his adult form and he was so strong if he held your hands you could not move at all.

Dennis loved his little brother Lynden and Lynden seemed to have total tolerance towards Dennis and they would often laugh together, they seemed to have a great understanding together and Dennis was always working hard to make little Lynden laugh, often teasing him until Lynden was giggling like a good one. This was a lovely thing to witness in a house of little love from our dad and I felt sorry for Lynden who was born into this religion and this showed in later years, den however had washed his hands with Jehovah's witnesses it was not for him too much sitting still many times for 2 hours at a time and den was horrified every time we had to do this and there was many rows when he refused to go to meetings and when he was forced would sit there hard faced and hardly spoke to anyone, is this a good thing? We were being forced to do and forced to believe in this teaching of their religion is this fare? It may have been allright for dad but you cannot force it on other human beings if they did not want it and although Dennis was 14, he knew what he hated and this religion was it. Lynden was so young he knew nothing else and settled into being a Jehovah's Witness, Danny put up with it under duress but hated it most of the time and Dennis and Danny would often have arguments because they were under stress put on them by their dad.

A few years went by and it was always the same thing every week Mondays chores and out for a few hours with the lads then in by 9p.m. for reading of the text book, this was just like a diary and topics of Jehovah's witnesses in other countries this took about 45 minutes every single night of the week, Tuesday local meeting called the group meeting just down the road in Gwyneth Parkins house that took about 1 hour and a half then the text book so the lads never seen their friends that night. Wednesday only the text book so maybe out for 2 hours after chores after school. Thursday's 2 hours of meetings in Bridgend some 8 miles away and Danny would ride his bicycle there and back. Friday nothing except text book and Saturday mornings knocking on doors preaching the beliefs of Jehovah's Witnesses for around 3 hours then home and do your chores and out for a couple of hours. Sunday clean the rabbit's cots out around 12 of them then get ready for the meetings in Bridgend at 2 am again that lasted for 2 hours home and more chores and maybe 1 hour out with the lads and so on and so on and den would be fighting to get out of most of these every day with serious consequences that affected everyone in the family but more so for den. Den was by now getting cleverer and cleverer and more cunning he would often be so serious to get out of meetings then when he was out of sight smile all over his face and Danny would laugh at him and say "you cunning little sod den he will catch you one day" Den laughing out loud said "no he won't he is silly ha , ha, ha," and den was right dad let him get out of it I think so mum would not start on him and things would go on like this for a long time.

Den would do something on his own back then that was so clever to keep his dad off his back and was really doing Danny a favour also but den was left alone, he would clean out the rabbits hutches out and feed them when we were in the meetings and dad found this a real help and left den to his own devises, very clever, so how stupid was he then? Not that stupid as he worked this out on his own back.

Den was now 20 and Danny was 14 and both of them very rebellious towards their dad and kept out of each other's way, den became so very serious every time dad was around but very excitable when not around and I felt there was something missing in den's life but could not put my finger on it, after all now he was a young man and developed the same as any normal person except in his head but not that far behind. He was now clean and a clean-living man taking care of himself much more although he still looked scruffy never mind what you dressed him in but with a smile on his face that would make anyone forgive him for any defects he had.
Danny and Mel were seeing girls and by definition den should be doing the same at his age and it showed many times in his action and in his little face often looking on with total jealousy and Danny noticed this as Mel by now was living in Milford Haven and Married to a lovely woman that den liked very much also, Marice was a lovely woman with a heart of gold and all the family liked her very much especially Dennis and this showed when Danny had a girlfriend he liked very much her name was Eileen Matterson she was a very pretty blonde gorgeous woman and very young and Dennis would make a huge fuss of her also as she was local and Danny would see that Dennis was very fresh with her at times but Danny took no notice as he thought well it's only Dennis nothing will ever happen and not realising that this was making Dennis very sad because he was not the same and was watched every time he went near any woman for fear of what he would do that was so unfair to Dennis as he was as gentle as a lamb and never had any thoughts of rape or anything like this I feel he would if he had a girlfriend would just love her to bits and pieces.

Dad was getting more irritated by the way things were changing in the house and Mel was now out of reach and living his own life and I would say happy because he was too far away and I believe this was what Mel wanted to get away from dad's grasp although he would not admit it as I went to stay often with Mel for several years and it was never a problem as

I feel Mel understood what I was going through, however poor old Dennis could not escape ever, he was stuck there day in day out and this made his life more of a problem for him.

It was a year later and Danny left school and went to work in the coal mines and life in the household was about to change dramatically and this would affect everyone. Danny had finished his training in the coal board and about to go to work in the Ffaldau colliery in Pontycymmer around 5 miles up the valley and he started to rebel against Jehovah's witness religion as it was not for him and going to meetings was out. It all came to a head one day with dad arguing with mum and dad getting very vocal and his temper was at his limit and Danny stood up to him and said "right that's enough stop it dad I will not stand by and let you abuse my mother like this this bloody religion has gone to your head and making our lives a misery so stop it now and take your religion somewhere else we do not want it here no more " Dad seen red and then set upon Danny who is now a big lad and could look after himself as he towered over his dad then dad said "I am the head of this household so don't interfere or I will." Danny interrupted and shouted "or you will what? I am not afraid of you and have had enough of you threatening everyone her you have destroyed this family for long enough and I am fed up with your ways and leave it there now or I will start ok?" dad red in the face replied "I beg your pardon? I am not putting up with your nonsense get up the stairs I will deal with you in a minute" Danny looked dad in the face and said laughing " I don't think so I am nearly 16 and have had enough of this crap, I have had to put up with it all my life with you and those bloody Jehovah's witnesses it stops from today on, I want nothing to do with them and I think Dennis has had enough also so leave him alone too " Dad then said "well the door is over by there, this is my house and if your not showing any respect for me as the head of the house then it's time you made your own way in this world and if this continues I want you to leave it" next thing Den spoke up "yes you are horrible and not nice picking on me all the time I don't want to go to meetings all the time and you should leave me and mum alone from now on ok?" dad jumped at den and said "you keep your nose out of it mister and get and feed the rabbits before I put the slipper to you" Danny smiled and said "see what I mean you have got to hit someone at all times he is 23 now even if he is mentally handicapped he has more maturity than most people I know so why don't you give him a break for a change?" Dad then said "what I do in this household is nothing to do with you anymore and I think you should find somewhere to live if you don't like it the way it is run by me. "Danny's face said it all and he was about to say something and mum now crying shouted "oh for god's sake Ray you are determined to destroy this family, aren't you? I will not stand by and let you throw out my sons one at a time, Mel has gone to Milford to get away from you now you are trying to get rid of another son of ours, don't you care about anything besides bloody religion? Because if Danny is thrown out, I will be leaving next I mean it." dad stood by his word and replied "well so be it if there is just me and Dennis left here then it will be a house of god's choice and will be a god-fearing house, but I will not put up with bad behaviour here you will do as I say or off with you. "Mum is now crying profusely and Danny says in a loud voice "Dennis will have his own choice about that as he is over the age of consent and I think he will rebel also as he has had enough of bloody Jehovah's witnesses, you're a fanatic you are." Dennis put his fist in his mouth seeing mum crying and said " yes I am going with mum or you must go to live in the Kingdom Hall she is my mum so leave her alone " dad then approached Dennis and give him a clip around the ear and in a nasty voice said " right you go and feed those rabbits and move it now please or I will get the slipper to you" Danny "typical more violence to your own son again, don't worry about me I am off I will not put up with this rubbish any longer and if I hear you have ever put your hand on mum I will be sorting you out old man, so remember I said that as I will not put up with it anymore " with that Mum started crying even worse than ever and in between her crying Dennis stormed out and mum said "oh no Danny don't be like that I can't let you go you have not got anywhere to go and this is your home please don't go, now stop it Ray he is only young" dad said " well he seems old enough to abuse his father's rule here so he can go if that is the case but he won't go anywhere as he needs to be in his mums pinafore and he will not have anywhere to borrow money off " with that Danny turns on his heels and goes up the stairs to pack a few things in his duffle bag and mum starts screaming at dad a real upset that day and yes Danny left the house and went to live rough in the Garw valley near his place of work.

Chapter 6

A sign of the times

Times became devastating for the whole family from this day onward or at least for 2 months and Danny came home a few times every week to see his mum and brothers as dad was in work and he could see how this was all affecting his mum Dennis and Lynden.

Well Danny was at home a lot lately as he was always down to see his girlfriend Eileen across the road and he came home one day and Dennis was so happy to see him and was full of fun with Danny that Danny had never seen in him before and Dennis run up to Danny smiling from ear to ear and rubbing his hands together profusely and said "hi Dan, how are you? And where are you living now? Mum has been crying as she is worrying about you and I am not talking to dad because he made you go away and Lynden is not happy either, so when are you coming home?" Danny smiled back at Dennis and said "wow, wow, slow down den, ha, ha, let me get a word in, have you been good?" Den with cunning smile says "oh yes" Danny "have you been looking after mum and linden?" "Yes, I have and the rabbits on my own and linden is now helping me when he comes home from school and he has been crying because he does not like sleeping in his room on his own and asks mum when you are coming back" next thing Mum walks into the room and a huge smile came over her face and she cuddles Dan and says "hello are you allright? I have been worrying about you and not been able to sleep are you ok?" Danny replies "yes I am fine but knackered and I have been offered a room with a friend in the Garw valley but not keen on doing it" Mum still smiling says "well you don't have to I have had it out with your dad and you can come home now or else I am leaving with den and linden and dad never questioned it at all he has realised he can't treat people the way he has" Danny serious face says "oh I don't know he will think he has won and I am fed up with his ways lately and will not live the way he wants me to so I will think about it" Mum smiles and says "fancy some apple tart and some tiesan lap cake?" Danny's face lit up and he jumps at the invitation and so did den who was so pleased to see Dan, Den says "if you come home I will let you borrow my new radio I bought anytime you like" Danny says feeling honoured by den's suggestion as den never lets anyone borrow anything off him says "well ok thank you den fancy going picking blackberries tomorrow for mum to make some tarts?" den rubs his hands together and says excitedly "oh yes we can go down near Shwt in them fields there as they have got huge blackberries there, ok I will be ready and dad will be shocked having blackberry tart, won't he?" Danny agrees and den asks him If he wants a cup of tea and Danny agrees. Dan said "well mum I want to come home but I fear dad will make it hard for me to settle back here what do you think?" Mum serious face replies "you don't have to worry about him I have had enough and he can see it and if I left him he would be finished and he knows it as he would not be able to show his face with his witness friends as he would feel a liar and he could not take that so just concentrate on coming home again and getting on with your life with Eileen she is lovely and misses you being nearby and you can see how Dennis misses you" Dan "yes I am shocked about Dennis being so nice to me and here he is with my cup of tea, thanks Den nice cuppa" Dennis gives a lovely laugh and huge smile and said "I am good at making tea aren't I mum?" mum says "yes you are den and have you missed Danny?" den not knowing what to say brushes his hair to one side which he always does when embarrassed says "yes he should come home and dad can go and sleep in the power station instead ha, ha, ha." Danny says "oh dear den that is your dad you are talking about ha, ha, ha." Den smiling says "I know he is a pain lately so he can sleep somewhere else and we can have some fun now" Dan then says "I will come home after this weekend if I have no problems with dad and linden will be happy not sleeping on his own aye?" den rubs his hands together he was so happy and mums face said it all and she smiled in a way that made Dan almost come to tears. Dan left before dad got home from work but Dennis could not resist telling his dad that Danny had been there, he said "Danny has been here to see us and we are going to pick some blackberries tomorrow down Shwt and we are going early." Dad replied "oh right, is he ok then? And you had better get to bed early if you are going blackberries picking as Danny likes to go early and he will probably get some wild mushrooms also knowing him." Dennis smiles and says "Yes I know he always goes early doesn't he and Wyndham is coming too, I hope it does not rain." Mum says "the weather forecast says it is going to be nice tomorrow." Dennis excited rubs his hands together and says "I have fed the rabbits so I am going to listen to my radio in my bedroom ok?" dad says "so it is still working is it Den? you have broken 5 radios and record players this last year so look after this one ok?" Den runs off to listen to his radio and it went silent in the living room between mum and dad both waiting for the other one to say something about Danny coming home then Mum says "He is thinking of coming home as long as you don't milk it and you had better not as I will be off if you do and I mean it" dad looking very sheepish says "as long as he lives by my rules I will be ok with it." mum snaps "we have had enough of your rules to last us a life time so don't keep on as long as he does not cause any trouble here you will leave him alone as he is a young man now and you must keep up with the times Ray or you will end up on your own you are like Hitler and we have all had enough of it." Dad walks out and mum had a little smile on her face.

Next day Danny turns up around 7am and Dennis was ready to go and Lynden ran up to Danny and hugs him and says "I hear you are coming home, aren't you?" Danny with smile replies "we will see how the land lies first but maybe." Lynden smiles and says "I am not coming picking blackberries it's too early for me to go out but I can't wait to have some blackberry pie." Next thing Dennis turns up with overcoat on with 2 large tins for the blackberries and he says "here you carry one, are you picking any mushrooms too?" Danny "I have got a plastic bag in my pocket in case we see some." Dad walks in and says to Danny "allright Danny boy see if you can get some Mushrooms as I got some bacon eggs and laverbread here for later, I am out on the ministry knocking doors this morning but we can have this for lunch and Dennis don't forget to clean them rabbits out later ok?" then dad went off to have a shave and mum says to Danny "I think things will be allright from now on but don't rub him up the wrong way mind." Danny laughs and says "I never rub him up the wrong way it's just the way he is mum." Mum smiles and tells Dennis "try not to get any maggots on those blackberries den and stay near Danny at all times ok?" Dennis says "mum I am a big man now so don't be silly." The lads went off for the day.

Well the lads got near the fields where they were about to pick blackberries and there was a gate, they would normally open easy but this time it was locked and Dennis would not climb over it and started to panic and Danny says to him "C'mon Den it is easy to get over, don't be nervous it is not going to bite you." Dennis looking nervous says "it's too high I will fall and there must be another way or I am going home." Danny tutted and realised that Dennis was not going to be able to get over this gate so they went down the fields a little to where there was a barbed fence he was able to climb through and as he was getting through he got caught on the barbs of the fence and Danny tried to help him Dennis by now was panicking and says "look now, I am stuck on this wire so help me as it's your fault." Danny was laughing and said "lift your leg and I will untangle you ok?" Dennis now started laughing and he lifted his leg and fell over and Danny fell on top of him and they were both lying there moaning and Dennis then said "you idiot I have ripped my trousers and I will be in trouble when I get home now because of you." Danny still moaning then starts to laugh and Dennis also started laughing at Danny and Danny in between laughs says "I can see your hairy leg and it is as white as milk let the sun get at it." they both got to their feet and brushed themselves off and den seen some mushrooms by his feet and told Danny about them and Danny said "they are not Mushrooms den they are puff balls and if we ate them, we would be very ill lets walk back to the blackberry bushes, oh look I can see some mushrooms over there now let me pick them to make sure they are mushrooms ok?" they both found mushrooms and then went to pick blackberries and there were loads of large blackberries and soon filled their tins after about 3 hours. It was nice to see 2 brothers getting on so well and they even found some hazel nut trees and filled up their pockets with nuts.

Well they got home and they were both very tired and mum was so pleased by the things they came home with and living in the village of Bettws was a bonus if you liked fresh wild produce and that's why Danny and Dennis loved living there. Mum made 5 lovely large tarts and Danny cooked up the bacon, eggs, Mushrooms and some lovely Laver bread which is seaweed so beautiful and full of vitamins and they all sat and ate it all up and you could see by dads face he was impressed and thoroughly enjoyed his feed and after Danny and Dennis shared out the nuts and dads eyes lit up as he loved eating nuts and for tea they all ate lots of blackberry pie with custard, what a fantastic day and Dennis and Danny fell asleep on the arm chairs for an hour and for a change dad and Lynden went up and fed the rabbits to let den have a snooze, is dad changing at last we will soon find out but mum had a massive smile on her face for a long time to come and yes Danny moved back in to his old room.

Dennis was now becoming a young man even though he had the mind of someone around 25 years his junior, but did he? Danny seen lots of improvement in him along with Mel as Mel said to dad on a visit home one day "well dad I think Dennis is becoming a lovely lad all of a sudden as see a difference in him as I have not seen him for 10 months a lovely lad isn't, he?" dad answered after thinking about it a while "yes I suppose so you may see it more than me as we are together all of the time and you as you said haven't seen him for a long while and I think he is more happier than I have seen him while growing up, I just hope it's the future for him as he has had a torrid life so far but he is mid 20's now and no one expected him to live for to see his first birthday." Mel continued "I was speaking to him when I arrived and he came bounding out to meet me and so excited with a huge smile from ear to ear." Dad's face went serious and he said "well I hope he will be happy after next week as he had got to go to Hensel Castle for a visit after 3 years and you know how he hates that place and I am dreading it and your mum is not happy either" Mel's face dropped and he tutted and said "oh dear he will be fuming when you tell him and he is a big lad now, what if he refuses to go?" dad "that's what I am afraid of he is so strong now I could never hold him and I am still trying to decide how to handle it as your mum will give in immediately so look out." Mel "rather you than me and he does not have a clue, does he?" dad says "no" then here comes Dennis smiling as he has been cleaning Mel's car and he is soaking wet from the waist down and Mel says to him "Hi Den did you manage to get any water on the car as you have most of it on you?" Den scratches his ear and laughing says "no I need some more water as this sponge got me all wet ha, ha, ha." Dad says "do you want me to put the hose up for you to use instead or does it need some more soap on It first?" Den with serious face says "another bucket of soapy water first then the hose please dad." Mel went off with den to get the soapy water and dad went up to the shed for the hose pipe to set it up for him. Dennis enjoyed washing Mel's car and tried to start up some fun with his dad by squirting water over him and dad laughing ran away and the fun began with the water. Den was already soaking wet and he was determined to get dad and Mel wet also. Den did eventually get them wet and laughed for hours and dad was getting cross so it all come to an end and Mel and Marice went home to Milford haven and den was a little sad after they went.

Dennis was puzzled for the next few weeks and one day made excuses not to go to the centre and this was the case now at all times he seemed as if he had lost interest in working in there and I was watching things as they went along and dad was not impressed he was not attending the centre but I think Dennis had found the centre now a little boring and wanted to stay home and lovingly wanted to help mum around the house without question with no moaning ever. Had Dennis seen things differently at home with mum as I noticed it but not dad he was only interested in his religion and I one day realised that mum was not that well in herself. She seemed a little vacant at times and was falling to sleep very often on her favourite armchair often with her head totally bowed to her chest and really fast asleep, she was struggling to do her house work and I noticed she bruised easily and her weight increased vastly and I could tell she was not the very fit mother I have always remembered all my life and I think Dennis was seeing this also and considering he was supposed to be mentally handicapped it was amazing how he picked up on it and in the end he would help mum in the day and go up the shop every day for her and was a huge help as mum was getting worse, is this the arsenal coming back to haunt her is she suffering due to the work she carried out in the war making bombs ? it surely was and it showed she became more immobile as the years were going on and Dennis was her rock most of the time he now did not attend the centre in the day and never went to meetings with dad he was standing up for himself and was not having nothing to do with anything he did not want to do. I felt Dennis was not as stupid as people made him out to be especially dad and Den did not give a damn what dad thought anyway, good for him although he spent most of his time in his bedroom window with a notepad in his hand making notes that only made any sense to him. Mum would use Dennis to help her with anything she could not do easily such as one day I witnessed her using a hoover and she wanted to separate the hose and make it shorter so she could get to corners easier and she called Dennis and said to him "oh den I can't pull this pipe apart will you do it for me and suck up the dust in the corners" and den with huge smile just done it with a lot of loving care. Mum was now in her late forties and this was not good as she was still so young and dad was not much help most of the time as nothing would get in the way of his religion.

I was still in the coal mines and not enjoying it very much a dirty dangerous place to be and I felt I needed to get out of there as soon as possible and I finally met a girl and moved in with her and her family but often went up to see mum and felt if I was gone at least she would have less work to do and I remember mum with fondness as she was a lovely woman and did not seem to have much of a life with dad but Dennis was always there for her never mind what. I felt a let-down for mum as I was only concerned with my future and in later years would often break out in tears thinking about what I could have done more for her but did not and I felt ashamed most of my life in later years but good old Dennis was always there for her never mind what he would not forsake her ever.

Dennis just got on with his life and helping mum a lot and now Lyndon had to do much more with dad's rabbits and his garden but he was the youngest and was never made to do it like myself and Dennis in earlier years and eventually dad gave up his rabbits as Lyndon showed no interest at all and Dennis stood his ground and helped his mum only. It was brought to the fore front one day when dad was home from work and not very well and Dennis was helping mum with the house work when dad said to Dennis "you can help me later Den to go up grandad's house for some coal with the motor bike and sidecar ok?" Dens face said it all as he was cleaning the stairs down and he replied "you will have to ask mum as we do the cleaning today and washing, I am too busy and mum needs me here ok?" dad said "I need help to do this so it will not take us long and then you can help your mum ok?" Den scratches his ear and comb's his fringe to one side with his fingers which normally means he is not happy and he then said "just get the bags on then fill them up and I can help you off with them when you get back you don't need me for that and me and mum are too busy, I am not coming up the Ogmore today am I mum?" mum nods her head as if to tease dad and Dennis and said "well it's too late now you should have mentioned it earlier and den is right we always clean up all day on a Tuesday ray so sorry we just can't change it just for you, den needs to be told the day before   " Dad stamps his foot and replies "ok then we will have to freeze here then" mum replies " well you never ask him to help when it is to do with the witnesses do you, you all help each other but when it's you who needs help you don't see any one of them do you? So, den will be helping me and that's that ok? "dad storms off to get his bike set up and mum smiles at Dennis then Dennis said "we are too busy mum, aren't we? Ha, ha, ha, he is not happy and grandad will help him anyway and they have got all day let's get on with it mum I want to listen to my radio later." Mum teases him "ok den I will jump for you now after you have made me a nice cup of tea, what do you think?" den tuts and makes a cup of tea for him and mum and as they were sitting down drinking them dad walks in and seemed cross and said to Dennis "so where's my cup of tea then? Didn't you make me one? Typical of you lot "den laughs and combs his fringe with his hand and dad was by now fuming and shouted at Dennis "I don't think it's funny, it's like I don't exist here anymore "mum looks on as Dennis gets flustered and says to dad "I am not your slave am I mum? I am busy helping mum so you can make it yourself for a change or wait until you get up with grandad and he will make you a cup of tea" Mum chirps up "oh c'mon ray he did not do it on purpose he didn't realise you wanted a cup of tea " dad just stomped out and went up to grandads and Dennis laughed for a while until mum told him off saying he should have made dad a cuppa but Dennis just didn't care and so they got on with the cleaning. It seemed as if Dennis had grown up and was not taking any more slavery from dad and I think it was because Danny had left home and he seemed to know that Danny was a lot younger than him and he should be given the same consideration, he is getting a good head on his shoulders and things were changing in the household. This went on for a long time with no change in the house at all for about 15 years.

Yes, it was the day he was going to a visit to Hensol castle hospital and everyone was dreading it and, on the morning, Dennis was all dressed up ready which amazed everyone and he was very upbeat for a change and then dad said "do you know where we are going today Dennis?" Dennis with a serious face said "yes I am visiting Hensol Castle and I will not be there long as mum said we could go to the café in Pencoed on the way home and I will never be staying there ever." Dad looking puzzled "and you don't mind going there?" "No don't care I am too old for that place now and it will be a nice drive up there and mum said I was to be a a good boy and I will get a new radio if I am good as the one I got is broke" Dad smiles and says "oh another broken radio, last week you broke the radio gram and also the television, you must stop messing with all these things den I can't afford to fix them all of the time so cut it out" Den smiles and walks off and mum came in and said to dad "he is happy to go there and it will be the last time he will be going there, I mean it I will be telling them today and that's that." Dad looked at mum then said "yes ok, I agree this is a waste of time and he is happy as he is so I will back you up Eileen, ok?" mum looked visibly shocked and said "right, I am glad we have got that clear and can we call in Pencoed for a cuppa on the way home as I promised Den, I would get him a toasty sandwich and a cup of tea." Dad agrees and off they went.

Well they arrived at Hensol Castle and it seemed different somehow and there was not a murmur from Dennis and they went into the reception and sat down and you could see Dennis visibly shaking with nerves and dad said to him "Dennis are you allright there young man." Trying to get him to settle down and Den just looked down to the ground looking upset and mum then chirped up "it's allright den there will be no problem, if they are not kind to you, I will take you out immediately ok?" Dennis smiled and agreed but still never said a word then dad said "if they seen him immediately that would be better for his nerves, but we always have to hang around." Mum smiled and said to Dennis "c'mon den we will go next door and have a cup of tea and dad will wait for them to decide when they want to see you, is that ok Ray? And then if they still haven't seen him when we have finished you can go with him to have one, what do you think?" Dad "do you think it's ok to do that? I don't know, ok I think it's fair as they don't seem to move very fast." Mum and Den got up and went for a cuppa. They had just gone for about 5 minutes and a woman called out Den's name and dad shouted "it's my son but he has gone for a cup of tea as you were so long." The elderly nurse snapped at dad "well we haven't got all day to wait for him you know he should be here waiting to see the doctor, it's not good enough Mr Duckfield just go and get him." Dad looked amazed at the way she spoke to him and said with serious face "what no pardon or thank you, I think you should talk a little better to me to get any response because I will not be talked to in that manner." The nurse then said "well he should be here waiting for the doctor to call him I will have to let someone else go in now and you will have to wait." Dad then said "fine you let me know when he will be seen then and I will go and get him and if it is not in the next hour, I will be off with my son and my wife to our home, I will not be hanging around here after that ok?" The nurse looked at dad in shock and then said "you can't go anywhere until he has been seen sir." Dad smiled and replied "I don't bet, but do you want to bet?" and the nurse stormed off and within five minutes she was back and in a mild-mannered voice said to dad "Mr Duckfield, is it possible to go and get Dennis and take him to room 2 please as soon as you can as the doctor will see him now, thank you." Dad sarcastically replies "of course my dear I will do it immediately, thank you." dad got up and went and got Dennis and mum and they all went into see the doctor who sat there stern faced and after a few minutes said "Ah Dennis Duckfield, how are you then?" den looked at mum and dad and never said anything and dad said "ok Den answer the doctor he will not bite you." Den smiled and said "yes ok." The doctor then said "so how have things been with him then?" Mum said "he has been fine no problems at all, thank you." Doctor "I see he has stopped attending the centre in Aberkenfig, any reason for this?" dad replied "he has out grown it and it is impossible to get him to go there anymore and he decided to stay at home and help his mother instead." Doctor looking serious says "do you think this is wise and is he capable of making his decision himself seeing how his mental mind works?" mum dives in before dad could say anything "why not he has matured a lot since his 24 birthday and we cannot force him to do anything he does not want and he is happy the way he has decided to run his life these days and he is a fantastic help." DR "; Yes, he maybe but you must let him know what is wrong from right, he just cannot make up his mind to suit himself he has learning difficulties and must be prompted in everything he does before any problems arise." Mum went to say something and dad chirped in Eileen I will sort this out if you don't mind, I think I know my son where as you see him every few years and in my mind I would not let Dennis do anything that will cause any problems ever, I want him to have a life also not live like a monkey in a cage he needs a life too and we are providing it for him and letting him make decisions for himself but keeping an eye on everything he does. My goodness he is a human after all and I will not let him be punished because he is mentally backward so do your best, we shall not be bringing him back here ever again so I wish you a good day sir we are out of here, goodbye, c'mon Eileen and Dennis let's go for a drive to Pencoed for a visit to that café for some sandwiches and tea." The doctor then gets aggravated and says to dad "you cannot just walk out of here just like that; I have not finished with you yet." Dad replies "as I said to that ignorant nurse, I do not bet but do you want to bet? We are off." Den had a smile on his face as he looked at mum and mum shrugged her shoulders and just followed dad out with the doctor looking dumbfounded by it all.

It was outside they were getting ready in the motorbike and sidecar and Dennis was scratching his ear and laughing and said "nice one dad you told him, he thinks I am stupid, don't he? But I have grown up to be a nice lad, haven't I? and that doctor had better watch out aye." Mum and dad started laughing out loud at what Dennis said and den then started laughing and pushing his fringe to one side and then slapping his legs as he laughed and they shot off to Pencoed for a coffee and hoped he would be happy at last. This day was a turning point in our lives as from that day den seemed settled with his life but it was not the end of Hensol castle or at least the doctors trying to interfere with dens life.

It was in the café in Pencoed that they bumped into aunty Mabel and uncle tony who had arranged to meet up with them and as they came into the café Dennis started rubbing his hands together profusely and a massive smile came over his face and he got up to greet them very excitedly and said "oh look who it is, ha, ha, ha, so what are you doing here ha, ha, I have been to Hensol and dad nearly beat up the doctor there and I have not got to go back there ever again isn't it mum?" Mum "no you haven't had you? You are very excited, aren't you? "uncle tony then said "well you are a big boy now see den aren't you and your father are fed up driving up there every so often aren't you Ray?" dad smiled and agreed with him then Mabel said "Eileen there is a new wool shop just by the monument, you should go and have a look there they sell off left over wool there cheap." Dad's eyes rolled and he said "Eileen you could sell them some wool the amount we have got in our bedroom so we will not be calling in there we have got enough ok?" mum just looked at dad with a smile and den asked "can we stop on the mountain for ice cream and see the sheep?" Dad said "don't be silly we are not going anywhere near that mountain we are going to Bettws den you can have some here as you have been good, right you go and get it here's the money." Den looked so uncertain but went up to the counter nervously and the lady said to him "right young man what can I do for you?" den muttered to her "can I have an ice cream please?" but the lady did not understand him and said to him "pardon I did not understand what you said sweetheart." He asked again but she did not understand him again and so mum said "sorry he has got a speech defect he wants an ice cream please "the lady smiled at Dennis and gave him an ice cream and gave him a little bit more than she should have and said "there we go my lovely a bit extra on there but don't tell anyone ok?" Den's face lit up and he left the counter without any change but the lady brought it over to him and then said to him "you will get fat with all that ice cream" they had a fantastic day by all means and it was nice to see Den having a nice time for a change and the sun was fantastic all that week.

It was the Sunday and Dennis was out feeding the rabbits and dad was in his meeting, mum was preparing Sunday dinner and next thing in comes Danny and his girlfriend Eileen Martinson a very slim pretty young girl with blonde hair and Danny was very proud of showing her off and she was a very excitable girl a few years younger than Danny and she loved Dan's mum and Dennis would always get excited to see her. Well next thing Danny was messing with the stereo and trying to play some Beatles music but it sounded awful and Danny tried to mend it when Den came in and seen Eileen and went up to her and rubbed her shoulders and said "hello when did you get here? I seen you yesterday up by the shops on your horse, but I am afraid of horses so stayed out of his way ha, ha, he is big." Eileen smiles at Dennis and teased him "I am bringing him over here tomorrow and you can feed him with some grass, I will show you what to do ok?" den scratches his ear nervously and says "oh I don't know he will bite me I think" Eileen smiling even more at what he says "no he won't I will be there and will show you how to do it and he will not bite you honestly." Dennis rubs his hands together and says "oh I don't know we will see. Hey Danny I can't get that stereo working properly I tried last night it's going funny." Danny looking annoyed says to him "it's broken that's why and I knew you had something to do with it the needle is knackered and I bet you had something to do with it didn't you and wonder what happened to my radio in my bedroom that is not working either, I have even changed the batteries and its knackered and I think you did it again." Den stops smiling and gets serious and says "hey I didn't do anything to the radio I have not touched your bloody radio and the needle was already broke on the stereo before I touched it and I will tell dad about you when he comes in right?" Danny snaps "it's always you that breaks these things here; you have broken about 10 things in this house this year alone, I will take the money out of your savings if it carries on, do you understand?" den snarls "you had better watch it I never done anything so shut up now." Danny was about to start ranting when Eileen says "oh c'mon stop it you two your brothers you should not be fighting all the time." Danny fuming says "well he is breaking TVs, radios, and now the bloody stereo it's got to stop den." Den biting his fist and looking mad says "you had better watch it or I will sort you out." Then they both started arguing out loud and mum came in from the kitchen and shouts at the both of them "right you pair stop it now I mean it or I will bang your heads together mind." Lots of moans and groans were heard from the brothers and Eileen says to mum "that's right Mrs Duckfield you tell them ha, ha, I bet you would sort them out too." Mum tuts and replies "boys they are always arguing and it gets me down and their father is no help he just makes it worse. Right Dennis that's enough now upstairs out of the way you can see Eileen later she will let you know when her and Danny leave ok? you pain in the ass." She smiles at Dennis and makes him laugh by pulling a face at him and off he trots muttering all the way upstairs to annoy Danny. Danny says "Eileen don't encourage him and scraping up to my mum it works with me mind. We are off to the shops mum do you need anything up there?" Mum replies "no Dennis got it earlier but thanks anyway dinner is about half past five Eileen are you eating with us or what?" Eileen answers "oh thanks for asking but mum always cooks around that time also and she has made me mine but thank you for asking." Mum "no problem I always cook too much I will see you later then, ta, ta, ta." They both go and say goodbye and Denis shouts "so long "they both scream back to him wishing him goodbye.

A few minutes later mum came in the lounge and sat down looking ill and gasps for breath and sits there with her head in her hands, things were on the turn with mum's life and health she became tired all of the time but tried never to show it and often fell asleep on the chair and just then in walks Dennis and says "ok mum? Are you tired I will make you a cup of tea if you want one?" Mum smiles and realises Dennis was no idiot he could see mum was not a well woman and often looked after her when all were out not realising, she was not well. Mum was dying due to the war effort by making bombs in the arsenal in Bridgend underground and often under the threat of German bombers trying to seek them out and in them days they never had health and safety she would not wear a mask in them days just breathed in all the chemicals including sulphur that would eventually kill her eating her from inside out even her hair turned yellow but no one noticed this happening for some years. Dennis seemed to sense that something was wrong and stuck to mum like a leach it was amazing how he knew. Well mum fell asleep before finishing the dinner and den kept an eye on it as best as he could and nothing got burnt and, in the end, mum finished it off and no one knew any better.

It was from that time on a lot of things started to happen in our household and not for the better, Danny got into lots of trouble with different things like girlfriends and getting into trouble with a particular family in Carmarthen and him and Eileen surprisingly parted to everyone's shock, lost his job with the NCB etc. Lyndon was growing up and went off the rails a little and Dennis just got lazy and unruly and it was just then a letter arrived at our home and it was from Hensol castle for mum and dad and all hell was about to be let loose after Mum read this letter and she just put her head in her hands and wept until dad got home from work and they waited until Dennis had gone to bed before dad read it and it said. Dear Mr Mrs Duckfield it was with great regret that you walked out on the appointment with Doctor George on the 14th of this month and we feel that nothing was resolved about the future of your son Dennis Duckfield and we feel it is important to make a home visit to discuss this problem in more depth. As a committee of member doctors we feel Dennis has not been given time to satisfy us that he is of good conduct and can behave in a normal manner due to him not doing certain things to make us feel he is safe to live in the public domain and so we have decided to carry out these tests in your home as a matter of urgency and would hope you would co-operate with these conditions and we would like you to get in touch on the telephone us on the number at the top of this letter to arrange this. yours sincerely Doctor H George.

Mum and dad just sat there for a few minutes and said nothing then mum sounding upset said "Well say something Ray, don't just sit there we need to sort this out permanently now it's getting me down and I will swing for them if things don't change." Dad tries to calm her down and in a calm voice says "Yes your right, it has gone on too long now and we need to get some closure on this matter of Dennis future, we both know he will never leave home and live alone or even get married and we have got no trouble with that and I think he is getting better all of the time with all the problems we used to have he keeps himself clean no more filling his pants and he is becoming a lovely lad. So, we must let them know he will be ok living his life with us until one day he has got to go into a home with people like him after we have gone agree?" Mum "That goes without saying and he will never cause any grief he knows the difference between right and wrong and we must convince them of that fact and get them to leave him alone for the rest of his life." Dad says "Right we both agree and will let them know how we feel and get them off our backs once and for all, so let's have some supper and forget about this until the day comes as we know what is going to happen so let's hear no more about it." Mum smiles and agrees with dad and they had a lovely supper and went to bed.

Well the day came around and the do gooders turned up and it was amazing how Dennis took the situation and he smiled and said to mum "I know all of those people why are they here mum I am not going to Hensol castle again and I am going to tell them." Mum says "No den we have sorted it out and will be telling them today before they start ok?" they all sit down and Dr George says "Well here we are again and I hope this is going to be productive today and we can sort out the future for Dennis, so how has he been this past 2 years I know all about the centre and." Dad butts in "I am glad you brought this up we are satisfied with his progress and need some closure on this we can't go on like this every couple of years he is fine I tell you." Mum almost in tears says "Yes he is and he is a fantastic help here in the house and I have now got a under active thyroid gland and his help is needed now." Dr George says "I am sorry to hear this and I assure you this is what this meeting is all about I agree that he more use to you at the marital home and I and the committee agrees with this so that is covered." Mum and dad looked physically shocked and smiled and the doctor continues. "Now we need to get money for him to support him in his adult life and there is lots of help in the government for his condition and we must get these forms filled out and signed ok? Also is he on any sort of medication?" Mum nods no and he continues "Can I and the committee do anything else to help you to make his future any better?" mum and dad sat there thinking and could not think as it was all too much all in one go so dad said "Can we think about this for a day or 2 please?" The doctor replies "Of course, no problem I have employed a helper on the other end of the telephone to do anything she can to help so I will give you her details on some paper, we are here to help not interfere but will always be on the end of a phone to do this and except for filling out these forms I have concluded our meeting." Mum and dad did not know what to say or do and so they got on with the forms and you could see Dennis's face light up and smiles all around.

After the doctor leaves you could see Dennis dying to ask a lot of questions and so he did "have I got to go to Hensol castle again?" Mum smiling says "No you haven't but you must help me around the house a little more instead ok?" Dennis says "Oh ok, I can do this and I can wash dishes and make the tea mum." Mum "Brilliant that is a good start." Dad said "Well that was a turn up for the books, and we will be getting more money to help to look after him and it will be back dated that will come in handy." Dennis smiling says "Yes I can have a new radio now and maybe a small television ha, ha, ha." Dad gave him a stern look and replied "I don't think so you will have to stop breaking things here first we are fed up with all the breakages through you." Den turned and went upstairs and mum says to dad "Yes it will be handy, things are looking up for a change as we have never had much luck for Dennis." Dad "Your right we haven't have we? Maybe things are going to get better for us, flipping heck look at the time I will be late for the meeting." Dad ran off to get ready and mum sat back with a huge smile on her face for a change as if to say about time we had a bit of luck.

Things started to get better for the family and mum seemed settled with her illness and started to depend on Dennis much more for things like preparing food and things like mixing cake mixtures and rolling out pastry etc. as it got a bit too much for mum he went up the shop nearly every day for her and down the doctors surgery to pick up prescriptions etc. and he started to talk to more and more people and was sometimes described as a bit of a lad. Well many stories came back to me by different people about how Dennis made them smile at some of the things he got up to, like one day he went up the shop for mum and he always used his make believe bus to do this pretending he was driving it and followed the kerb all the way to the shop spinning his steering wheel as he went, changing gear and making the sound of a bus with his mouth even making the sound of air brakes etc. People got used to him doing this but Danny and Lyndon used to stop him if they ever seen him as they felt embarrassed, but back to the story, he drove his pretend bus up to the shop then known as Peggy's and he turned up in the shop and said to a total stranger "Excuse me do you know you have parked in my parking space?" the man looked at Dennis and replied "Oh I am very sorry I will go out and move it immediately for you, I and new around these parts, sorry." Dennis said "Oh ok I see, but I am sorry I always park there." The man then rushed out of the shop and Dennis followed behind, the man then got into his Cortina and moved it and closed the door and looked and seen Dennis with his pretend bus pull into the space put his air brakes on pretended to open the door got out pretend to close it and lock it, the man was baffled by this sight and did not know what to say and Dennis put his hand up and acknowledged to the man and said out loud to him "Thank you mister I just got it in there ta, ta," The man just stood there for a while and looked worried and Dennis went into the shop and done his shopping. Another time he was down in the doctor's surgery picking up some medication for his mum and he had his stuff and as he was going, he seen his neighbour waiting and said to her "I have got my taxi outside do you want a lift home in it?" It was Mrs Pope who lived across the road from us and she replied not thinking "Oh yes please I won't be long now." Dennis says "Ok I am parked outside and will wait for you." Mrs Pope then said "Ok I will see you out there in a minute and thanks for this." Dennis went outside to wait for her and after a few minutes she appeared outside looking for Dennis and seen him stand outside but no car was there and she realised it was all in Dennis mind and tried to make excuses for not standing by his side and pretend to be in his taxi and other people were in stiches with laughter and in the n Dennis pulled off and said to her "Ok see you again and don't be afraid to ask any time for a lift ta, ta, ta." Dennis had a character of his own and made many people smile with the things he did and the majority of the people in Bettws absolutely loved them and were not afraid of him at all.

Dennis and mum became so very close over the years and I think if anyone done anything to mum look out, he would sort them out, they done everything together and never a cross word and you could not say that about anyone else in Dennis's life he did not take fools lightly.   He was becoming a real gentleman in more ways than one but was still tormented by some of the younger generation of the village and Danny was always fighting his battles for him and Dennis was always telling Danny everything that went on in his life and often pointed to the culprits while Danny was confronted by them, it was like Danny was the older brother and Dennis would look up to Danny to sort out his troubles often with a huge grin on his face.

Dennis seemed a different man these days so understanding and so loving and was a real gentleman in many ways, always understanding many jokes and laughing along and could be very jovial with everyone, is this man who is mentally backward? I think he was just misunderstood and given the chance could be as normal as anyone else. Dennis was becoming very important to the family and did many things that went un-noticed like making tea for everyone and knowing who had how many sugars and no milk etc. going up the shop and realising how much change he had back and the goods he had to get for mum, giving messages in a correct way without forgetting and this was important to him. He was also paying attention to the opposite sex and not being a pain at the same time but showing total respect for them and not pestering them all of the time, a real gentleman but where would his life go from here a single man for the rest of his life we expected and what would happen to him when mum and dad left this earth? As Danny and linden and of course Mel will have their own lives to live and so what's going to happen to him?

Well it came the day when Danny left home and got married and there was now only linden and Dennis left in the family household and life was going to change but not for the worse.

Bettws was more welcoming to Dennis at last people took to him without fear and often had a lot of fun with him now they know him and lots of people fell in love with him. Bettws was a lovely village for the likes of Dennis to spend the rest of his life in and he was comfortable doing so and he kept himself very private and him and mum did lots of things together and dad left him to his own devices as long as it did not contradict his religious beliefs. Den had lots of love for music just like the other brothers, the Beatles, the Monkeys and so on and den still broke many radios, stereo players and televisions that made dad and mum furious but it was just in his way of life he could not help himself, for many years den was a happy man and the only thing I could tell he lacked was a woman in his life as he had the same feelings as any human and he many times looked lost on his own and often looked frustrated with life but he just got on with it as there was not much could be done for his problems. If only he could meet someone just like him and life would be complete for him as you could often see his problems in his eyes, I am surprised he did not go mad, and mum and dad were getting old and what would become of him if they passed away? It was something not to think about until it happened, what would become of him will his brothers take him in? Would he be happier in a home for people like him? God knows, it was a permanent worry for all concerned except Dennis he just plodded along without much of a care in the world.

CHAPTER 7

THE LATTER YEARS

Mum and dad were ageing fast as the years of the war took their toll on their health. Dennis was now in his late 30's and leading a boring life without any money worries or anything to concern him and he looked bored with life spending most of it in his bedroom looking out of the window with a writing pad and pen in his hand at all times, he often had young kids poking fun of him as they passed but den was starting to look old himself and the only contact he had was with his little brother Lynden who was now in his late twenties living home fixing cars for a living after leaving the coal mines and him and dad done lots of things together especially with cars as dad now had passed his driving test after Lynden kept on at him to do so and they both messed around with mechanics and dad took voluntary redundancy from the power station to go self-employed so he can become a pioneer for the Jehovah's Witnesses that he loved doing he also cleaned windows, swept chimneys for a living. Lynden had a drive made with a pit beside the house and Dennis was very interested in what his dad and Lynden was up to. Dennis was interested in cars and busses etc. and often went down the bottom site about a mile away and get a lift back up to his house with a neighbour Mr Morgan who had a lorry and came home every night at the same time and Dennis loved doing this on a regular basis, he also stopped playing at busses, he seemed to lose interest all of a sudden.

Mum was now getting house bound with her health and it showed and dad seemed to slow down all of a sudden also and never had the stamina he always had he struggled picking things up and he did however not let it beat him.

Dennis spent lots of time watching Lynden and dad working on cars etc. Lynden often tried to get Dennis involved but Dennis was just happy watching and making the tea, he did one day show Lynden, Danny, Gaffo and terry lambert up when they stripped off some callipers to put new disc brakes on the front of a car for a friend and they took it apart but forgot how it came off and all 4 of them puzzled for about 2 hours on how to get this back together. It was a lovely day so they all decided to have a beer and asked Dennis to watch the tools etc. for just a few minutes. Dennis agreed and stood there watching everything and the lads went in out of the sun for a cold beer, well about fifteen minutes went by and they all went back to work and all of them were stumped when they saw one of the brake callipers were back together and linden said to Dennis "who did this Den?" Dennis laughing all over his face replied "I did silly man, and you can do the other one I could not do that one the same." The lads were stumped as what to say but Gaffo then said "and he is supposed to be mentally backward and we 4 just could not work it out, that's bloody incredible." Danny and Lynden patted Dennis on the back and were very proud of him and terry gave Dennis a can of beer and Dennis looked so proud and felt grown up with his can and it took him all morning to drink it but made the most of it.

Another day he lost his temper with Lynden and they had to pushed a car up the slope to the pit in the side garden and it would not start and linden was shouting at him to push harder and Dennis lost his temper and gave it a good push with his mighty strength and pushed it too hard and pushed into a wall and gave Lynden some dents to knock out as well and Lynden never shouted at him again, and Dennis went around the corner of the house and laughed for ages.

Dad was seen less and less these days spending lots of time preaching as well as being self-employed but dad was loving his new life and all the boys were grown up now, less for him to worry about and mum was glad to see dad gone most of the day, less hassle in the house but dad was having trouble with his heart but never seen it creeping up on him until one day it happened and it was a huge shock to the whole family as dad never drank or smoked and ate very healthy he was in work sweeping chimneys in a place called Heol-y-cyw down the valley and had a massive heart attack and was rushed to hospital in Bridgend and things were about to take a massive turn in our family.

It was around lunchtime when a phone call came into mum saying that dad had, had an accident he had fallen and was taken into hospital in an ambulance and mum got very agitated on the phone and Dennis got very irritable hearing this and mum rushed out to tell Lynden who was repairing a car outside and she seen Dennis standing behind her looking very upset and she said to him "oh Dennis are you allright? Don't worry it's dad he has been taken ill and I am going to get linden to take us to the hospital in Bridgend, so go and change your clothes for me please." Dennis in a panicky voice said "why? What has happened to dad? I don't want to go to the hospital, I don't like hospitals." Mum looked at Dennis and screamed at him "this is not the time to play me up go and get ready now." Dennis stormed off after hearing this and mum still in shock went out to Lynden and he could tell the was something wrong and said immediately "mum what's wrong? What is it?" mum looking as white as a sheet replies "your dad has been taken into hospital he had a fall and they think he may have had a heart attack." Lynden says "ok don't panic let me change and I will run us down there now." Off they went to the hospital. Dennis seemed strange at the news of dad and sat silent in the car on the way down and just as their neared the hospital he sprang in to conversation "so what are they doing to dad then? Is he coming home with us later? Is he going to be allright I told him not to work with all that dust from the chimneys and I don't like hospitals I can wait in the car if you like" Lynden replied "calm down den it's ok and no you can't wait in the car you had better stay with us if you don't mind please, are you ok mum?" "I am fine thank you lets go and see how your dad is doing" They entered the hospital and found where dad was and the doctor spoke to mum "He is allright now at the moment but he has had a warning and he must slow down and take it easy I am afraid he will have to stop working even though he is very young his heart is in a bad way and if he does not listen he won't be with us much longer. So, can we get this into his head and prepare him for a restful life?" Mum and linden looked startled at what he said not thinking how serious it was and it certainly got through to the family.

By dad's bedside they joked with dad Lynden said "anything to get out of work aye? And I will get the car for you later ok? You have put the willies up us all now how are you feeling?" dad looking ill replied in quiet voice "allright now but still aching in the heart area I don't know what happened one minute I was working along then the next I was in an ambulance." Mum looking tearful said "well that's the last of your working days according to the heart specialist he says you must give up work immediately." Dad looking serious "yes he said this to me also but we will manage somehow, I will have to sign on disability this week that's all." Mum tuts and says "well I suppose you will be hanging around my ass from now on then, that's all I bloody need is a miserable git like you making my life a misery." You could hear a pin drop after mum uttered those words and then dad looked at Dennis who looked ill and said "allright den? Your quiet today, what's the matter?" Dennis shrugged his shoulders and laughed and said "nothing I am ok are you coming home later with us?" Dad says "no I will be spending some time here for the doctors to get me better." Den "ok I will look after the rabbits and clean them out" dad smiled and said "good man I knew I could rely on you and linden if you don't mind picking up my car and the equipment, I will rest better." Lynden agreed and said to Dennis "c'mon den lets go for a cup of tea and let mam and dad have a chat." This they did and sitting in the café Dennis said is dad ok Lyn? He looks awful. "Lynden looking worried replies trying to reassure him "yes den you know dad hard as nails it will take more than a heart attack to stop him in his tracks, so don't worry he just needs to take it easy from now on." Dennis smiles and brushing his fringe to one side he says "I know we can look after his rabbits and his garden for him to have some rest is it?" Lynden laughs and says "ha, ha, ha, we do that now not dad he just barks out the orders I think we should stop breeding rabbits for meat and let them go for pets and have done with it." Den's face went serious and he said "I don't think dad will let us do that he will go mad and I am not going to be there when he does, you can tell him." Lynden says "I will tell him I have not got time to look after them I got my own life to live and you can't look after them on your own, can you?" Dennis rubbing his hands together says "oh no I am not good at doing everything am I? And mum will not be happy with dad if he don't listen, will she?" Lynden "no she won't and he must realise things have got to change for the better, have you finished your tea? Oh yes you have lets go and see how things are with mum and dad."

They toddle back and mum and dad were having a serious chat and they were both smiling and mum says "hi lads ok? Your dad and I are working out how to go forward when he gets home." Lynden speaks up "oh yes, den and I have decided that we need to let the rabbits go as it is too much for me and him and I have got work and really haven't got the time and den can't work with them on his own they will be dead in 3 weeks." Dads face was a picture and he said "I have had rabbits for 25 years I can't let it go. "mum chirps up "well ray you will have to it's too much and there is no profit in it let them go we have got around 12 baby rabbits that can go to Maesteg market and sold for pets and the other can be kept for meat until they have all gone, ray it's the only way so don't make it harder than it needs to be."

Dad looks dejected and was sad but agreed and mum felt awful but it was the only way and the lads were surprised that dad gave in so easy, has this attack changed dad and now he realises he is not getting his own way from now on I suppose it is a great shock for him.

Later at home Dennis says "so we are getting rid of the rabbits then it will be funny not having rabbits in the shed first the chickens now the rabbits and soon all the gardening and no more vegetables ha, ha, dad will be miserable I think." Mum says "well it's for the best it's your father's hobby not ours he will have to fall in line now he is very ill. I am going to have a hell of a life now he will be under my feet, what have I done to deserve this I am not that good with my health either, who's going to look after me?" Dennis and Lynden says at the same time "we will look after you both, ha, ha, here is Dan allright Dan?" Danny looking flustered says "so how is he then I have rushed home as fast as I could but it has taken a time, phew." Lynden says "he is fine and now realises he has got to take it easy and get rid of the rabbits and slow down and he agreed to it." Dan looking amazed says "what he agreed to it, that is a turn up for the book he must be bad, and what did the doctors say?" mum said "he has got to give up work and look after himself not get into any rages, that's a laugh he has got a bad temper and that has not helped he will be a pain to get on with for a long time "Dan "well at least he is still alive that's the main thing pain or not he is alive we must get things sorted out here immediately before he gets home and changes his mind." Lynden "yes I will take the rabbits to the pet shop up to maesteg market day after tomorrow and we need to sort this house out a little get rid of the clutter and sort out everything to make his life easier." Dennis says laughing "I can do the stairs and do some hoovering and sweep the paths around here ha, ha, and mum says I can help with the cooking of cakes and that." Danny smiles and says "oh dear den I don't think dad will be scoffing cakes in the future he must eat a good balanced meal, although he already does so why the heart attack? He has always eaten fruit vegetables and never drinks or smokes or even drink coffee." Mum speaks up "exactly I said this to the heart specialist and he reckons it's his bad temper that has caused this and I don't wonder, he needs anger management and cool down so we must not wind him up at any time agreed?" They all agree and looked a little concerned and den especially looked worried.

Well dad came home a few days later and the rabbits had already gone and dad looked lost at home and was very quiet for the first few days and the lads did everything and watched dad at all times and the only thing dad was so concerned about was getting to meetings and for once he listened to his family and many of the witnesses came along to the house to see him and when they were there Dennis disappeared up the stairs. I think Dennis feared they would try and get him to go to the meetings again and he was clever enough to see through this, mum however just said yes to everything not really listening to them but dad was much better in himself when they called in to see him. Dad felt like a fish out of water and was watched by his family making sure he did not do anything strenuous especially Dennis he watched dad like a hawk and this showed in the weeks to come.

One day dad was walking around his gardens seeing nothing hardly being grown as dad never had lawns if it could not be eaten he would not grow it and his face told it all as life went on he still tried to look after a few cabbages, lettuce, etc. but he was failing fast and it was one day and den was following him around the gardens he seen dad trying to pull off some dying leaves of a cabbage plant and Dennis said to him "aye what are you doing? You are not supposed to be doing that, or walking around for long I will get mum." Dad said to Dennis with a grin on his face "Dennis you are getting on my nerves watching me all of the time, haven't you got something else to do? I feel like a rabbit caught in car headlights all of the time with you." Dennis rubbing his hands together and smiling from ear to ear said "you must not be doing anything or you will be ill and back in hospital, you are not good on your legs are you? And that walking stick is for you to help you not for moving things in the garden so let's go and sit in the house is it? And I will make us some tea." "Oh, Dennis stop it will you I am fine and it is a nice day to be in the garden so go away and leave me alone." Dennis laughed even more and realised dad could not do anything about him and den went around the corner for a second or 2 and dad said to himself "thank goodness he has gone he is like a leach on my back" just then den popped his head around the corner and said still laughing "I am watching you mind ha, ha, ha, don't do anything mind or I will tell the doctor ha, ha, ha." Dad sighed and said "Dennis you are getting on my nerves you know I am coming in for a sit down." Dad walks past Dennis and went in and sat down and mum was writing a letter and he came in muttering and she asked him "what are you muttering about? And who are you telling off?" Dad said "oh Dennis he is following me around and commenting on everything I do he is driving me crazy can't we send him back down to that centre he used to go to "den put his head inside the door and said "no I don't go there anymore I am too old ha, ha, I am going to make some tea shall I?" Mum chirped up with a smile and said "good idea den I could do with a cup of tea, and so what was you doing outside then

Ray to get Dennis to stop you." Dad replied with red face "nothing just having a look at my cabbage plants and you would think I was planting spuds the way he talked to me." You could hear Dennis in the kitchen pretending to sing with a lot of laughing going on in there and mum started to laugh then Dad also started to laugh and comment "see what I mean ha, ha, ha, he is driving me nuts ha, ha, ha." Mum "well shows he cares about you don't it?" Den brings in the tea for mum and dad and one for himself then mum then says "ray you must look after yourself you can't do what your used to it's not good for your heart so relax a bit more." Dad nods his head and sighs and puts some handles Messiah on to relax himself then Dennis shot up the stairs to get away from it dad smiles as if to say right I know what to do now play my music and den will leave me alone.

Next in walks Danny and he said "Hi all everything ok? I just popped in to see if I can do anything as I am having an early day from work." Dad in a miserable mood says "yes fine, I am a bit fed up with not being able to do anything and being watched by your brother Dennis who is getting on my nerves and by the way can I have a lend of that record you have got of amazing grace I love that song?" Danny said with confused face "Yeah ok, I will drop it up in the morning and you can have it if you like it is too morbid for me these days." Dad "Are you sure? I love that song since you played it here a few months ago never new it existed, thank you." Danny says yes of course you can have it, where's Lynden then? I was wondering if he fancies going up to the vets in Blaengarw tonight for a couple of sherbets." Mum says he has gone to fix a car for someone he won't be long as it is get in dark" den listening says "I fancy a few sherbets ha, ha, ha." Dan says I bet you do." Dennis laughs and said "I think dad needs a beer for his heart it will do it some good I bet ha, ha, ha." Dad smiles and says "I could do with a nice bottle of Newcastle brown I have not had a glass of brown ale for about 20 years but I would not stop at one so no thanks, mum looks as if she needs a good stiff drink." Mum "I have got some sherry in the cupboard and it is around 20 years old and I bet it is very strong now, I will give that to your dad to shake him up a bit." Next in walks Lyndon all covered in oil he smiles when he sees Danny and says "how's you bro?" Danny "allright Lyn fancy a couple of beers up the vets club tonight?" Lyndon smiles even more and says "do bears crap in the woods?" Dad rolls his eyes and mum laughs out loud and Danny goes off to change for later. Lyndon asks dad "how are you today and can you lend me £20 until tomorrow? Ha, ha, I am sorry but I am in a hurry." Dad says yes and Lyndon goes off to change and dad was starting to nod off to sleep and mum says to him "Ray why don't you go and have a lay down for an hour you look shattered." Dad jumps in his chair and says "oops I have not done a thing to get shattered I feel like I was about 100 years old these days I think I will read the bible for five minutes then if I fall off to sleep let me just sit here for a while ok?" Mum looking concerned says "yes ok are you allright? Do you need anything?" Dad nods no and Dennis gets up and makes him a lovely cup of tea that dad appreciates as you could see by his face. Dennis looks concerned also and worried very much as mum recognises and follows Dennis out to the kitchen and says to him "dad is not well den so don't worry we will look after him between us ok?" Dennis with sad face nods and mum felt lost in this all and the whole house was in turmoil about dads health and they all knew it was just a matter of time.

Dad's health got worse and his heart was failing fast and it was a sad time in the Duckfield household and everyone was on pins, Dennis was a worry as he was not taking dad's heart problems very well and was like a leach behind dad at all times. Well the day came when he had to go into the University of Wales hospital for heart surgery and things a few days before took a bad turn, dad insisted to his doctor that he will in no circumstances were they to perform a blood transfusion on him never mind what. He was sitting in the house with mum and Dennis present and the doctor and dad says "right doctor Davies I am going to request that no one in the hospital when I have the operation or any other time are, they to give me any blood ok? And that is final." Mum stared at dad and the doctor said "well we don't know what will happen in surgery it may become necessary Mr Duckfield I am sorry." Dad gets frustrated and says "I am a Jehovah's witness and it is against my faith to take any other person's blood as I will refuse to have the operation if I am not happy about things so I need your assurance about this matter." Doctor Davies and mum looked stunned and the doctor says "ok Mr Duckfield I must accept your request but I will speak to the hospital and the surgeon and tell them this and they will ask you to sign a form with your request on and that will be that, I am getting an ambulance to pick you up in the next 2 hours to take you in as a matter of urgency ok? I must get back to the surgery and make some telephone calls about this matter immediately, I however think you are a fool to take such risks but it is your choice, good day." The doctor left and it was mum's turn to have a go at dad "oh ray be sensible and don't rock the boat, you may have to have blood or die, don't be silly and stop thinking of yourself for a change." Dad now red in the face replies "Eileen it is my body and I will not go against my religious beliefs so let's leave it at that it's my choice." Mum gets up and walks out of the room and you could hear her cursing all the way up the stairs. Dennis was sitting in the room with dad not realising what this was all about and he looked upset and says to dad "so what are you doing are you going to die dad?" Dad puts on a smile for Dennis and says "don't be silly den I will be allright don't worry things will turn out allright and if not, I will be happy in heaven with Jehovah and we will see each other soon enough so look after your mum ok?" Dennis looked even more confused and kept on at dad "why? What do you mean? I need help to do it all here and Lyndon needs help with the cars so you must get better or we will not be able to get on with things." Dad smiles and says "everything will be allright you will see, any chance of a cup of tea before I leave den the tea in the hospital is not as good as what you make." Dennis rubs his hands together and says with a huge smile "ok dad no problem I will do it now." Den went into the kitchen and dad bows his head and nearly starts to cry as if to realise he will never see Dennis ever again and a little tear comes to his eye. Dennis gives dad a cup of tea and dad says "oh that's lovely den, you are the only one who can make me a fantastic cup of tea like this, so you are in charge now ok as you are the oldest here while I am in hospital." It was too much for dad and he puts his hand over his face and started to cry and Dennis just burst into tears and they were both sobbing uncontrollably and Dennis panicking says "what dad? What dad? Why are you crying? You have made me cry now and I don't know why? Are you allright shall I get mum?" dad pulls himself together and looks at Dennis and smiles and says "sorry, do you know how special you are to me and your mum, we have brought you up to be a lovely little man and if I don't come home from the hospital and you get upset by this please remember I love you very much and I am so proud of you and your brothers and look after your mum promise?" Dennis still crying says "you will be allright dad you will see I will look after your car ok? I will clean it regular and Lyndon will help me I will come up to see you in hospital and I will look after mum but remember we will go out for a few more walks when you come home." Next thing in comes Lyndon puffing like an old man and he says "wow what's the matter with you two? What's all the tears for?" dad and Dennis wipe their eyes and dad says "I am going into hospital for urgent surgery and I have told the doctor and mum that I will not be having any blood if it becomes necessary and mum and Dennis got upset and mum stormed up the stairs, I am just getting things in order if it comes to it." Lyndon looking sad says "oh c'mon dad it will be allright me and den will look after everything here so don't worry, we will all be laughing all about this this time next year you wait and see." Dad looking down to the floor says "I wish I was as confident as you son." Lyndon storms off to see how his mum is and Dennis sits silent as if he understands everything and the love in the air was incredible for once, mum came in with a bag of things for dad's stay in hospital and her face was red and you could see she had been crying and dad puts out his arms and she cuddled up to dad and they all started crying again and Lyndon stayed in the hallway as he did not want his dad to see him cry.

The ambulance turned up and dad walked out to the ambulance with Dennis, Lyndon and mum following behind, he got into the ambulance and was made to lie down and first mum gave him a hug and a kiss and said her goodbye's and then Dennis did the same and burst into tears, then Lyndon did the same but kept a cool and calm face and off he went. In the house Dennis went straight up the stairs and sobbed his eyes out as if he really believed he would never see his dad again and in walks Lyndon and Mum to comfort him but this was not the end of the sadness that was about to overcome the whole family.

Danny was the only one asked to go up to visit dad before the operation as dad needed as much peace as he could get and Danny arrived by his bedside and dad was reading the Watchtower a magazine by the Jehovah's witness and they greeted each other and Danny said "ok dad? I have brought my personnel cassette tape recorder so you can listen to some of your music while you are in here, how are you feeling?" Dad looking real tired says "bored and tired but thanks for the recorder it will be better now to be able to listen to my music, thanks, how is your mum?" Danny in serious face replies "getting on with it, but mostly in a daze, its Dennis I am worried about he is not happy you are in hospital so get well soon and let's get back to normal. Lyndon has gone serious as usual he cannot take pressure like this and never has been able to and Mel called me on the phone earlier and said to give you his love from all down in Milford, he sounded concerned also but he is a long way away, I expect he will come up over the weekend to see you, well he said that to me." Dad said "I am in for the operation tomorrow and the surgeon says it is likely I will hardly lose any blood and it will be fine, but I signed a piece of paper that I am not to have any blood transfused into my body never mind what, I want you to make sure they stick to it ok? Promise me." Danny looking awkward says " oh dear dad please don't put me in this situation if you have signed a piece of paper your wish will be carried out to the letter so I am not getting involved it's you and your bloody religion and it's crazy as far as I am concerned but I will not get involved, I will leave it up to Mel he is in your gang, sorry dad it's all getting to me and the whole family and it will not make me feel any better to go against your wishes, so let's leave it there now. What is the food like here?" Danny trying to change the subject "I don't know I am nil by mouth at the moment but it smells lovely and I could do with losing a few pounds ha, ha, ha." Danny says "I have never liked hospital food shall I bring you something nice from home after your op tomorrow night? Like some Welsh cakes and some loaf cake even some apple tart as mum has not stopped cooking since you came into hospital, I think she is putting a brave face on it and keeping herself busy and Dennis is helping her." Dad's face lit up and he was almost dribbling with the thought "oh yes please a bit of everything I have always loved your mothers cooking she is a wizard with food and stuff the weight ha, ha, oh I must not laugh too much they will think I like it here." Danny looks sad all of a sudden and says "your going to be allright and in a few days I will bring Dennis up to see you before he drives me mad with all the questions, he is really worried about you, you know I have never seen him like this before." Dad smiles and says "I know he has turned out to be a lovely young man, all those worries when he was born and most of his life and there was never any need to worry, he is champion I am looking forward to seeing all the family after this is all over." It came time for Danny to go and something very unusual happened dad stopped Danny just as he was about to set off and Danny sat on the edge of the bed and dad said with a tear in his eye "if this does not work out in the operation please make sure that you tell them all I love them and will see them in Paradise because I don't think I am going to survive this I am getting worse every day and I want you to know I have not always been right with you but you were a handful and I regret a lot of the ways I handled things sometimes you have not turned out too bad so look after them all and make them look after each other ok." Danny had a tear come to his eyes and he stopped for a while then said "don't be silly I will make that promise as long as you tell them after you come home instead." Dad promised and Danny left for home.

Danny got home to Bridgend and popped into see his mum to report and she was waiting up for him to call and let her know what his dad was like in the hospital "Hi mum, he is ok but worrying a little, he is acting funny as if he wants to die and go to heaven the way he talks it's annoying the way he is all god and nothing else, but he sends his love to you and he is having the operation around 11am in the morning and he will try to phone you early ok?" Mum smiles and says "yes ok, I think he has given up he is not the man I used to know he is ill and his belief keeps him going I suppose but I hope he will be allright, Dennis has been asleep since around 8 o'clock he is shattered as he has not slept for 2 days or more worrying about your dad, I will give you a ring in your work to let you know how his op went ok? I need to try and get some sleep myself as I keep on nodding off." Next in walks Lyndon half cut with the beer and smiles a silly smile and says to Danny "so how's the old man up there? All doom and gloom I expect he is upsetting everyone especially me and Dennis." Danny answers "a little bit I suppose but you know what he is like with his religion but he is having the op in the morning around 11am in the morning so I suggest you all get a goodnight sleep he is going to be a handful in his recovery, I am off speak in the morning.

The next day and mum had a call off dad and she spoke to him as normal and he was about to hang up and Dennis spoke to him "hi dad are you ok? I am helping mummy with cakes and tart for you and Danny and Lyndon says I can come up to see you tomorrow with them so be good and I will see you then." Dad replies "ok I look forward to it and be good for your mum ok?" Dennis agrees and mum says goodbye and wishes him luck with his operation. It was around 1pm the phone rang and mum answered and screamed out loud and there was mayhem there "oh god no, no,, no, it can't be true poor Ray why, why, I was talking to him an hour ago" surgeon on the end of the phone says while mum was crying uncontrollably " I am sorry Mrs Duckfield he was just too weak his heart had heart failure and it was just too much for him, he hardly lost a cup of blood so that was not the reason I am so sorry I will get someone to call you later ok?" Mum puts the phone down and in runs Dennis shouting at mum who was crying her eyes out "mum what's the matter? What is it? Why are you crying?" Mum still crying said to him "where is Lyndon, go and get him quickly." Dennis runs out to get Lyndon and in they both walk and Dennis was as white as a sheet, Lyndon says "oh no mum please don't say it it's not true please." Mum through her tears said "I am sorry boys but your dad died in the operation theatre he was just too weak and died." The both lads just burst out crying saying "oh no poor dad he knew he was not coming back." Dennis in total shock says" he will be home soon stop it he is not dead, so don't say that he is ok he told me he would be home next week oh no, oh no, oh." Dennis went into shock and threw himself to the floor, this made mum worse and Lyndon helped Dennis up and sat him onto the sofa and sat by the side of him and done his best to comfort him "C'mon den calm down please, dad did not want to die but that's life den, please calm down." Dennis in a sad state of mind says "no, no, no, he is not dead he is coming home soon, please mum lets go up and get him home he is not dead your lying, he needs us to look after him." Next thing Lyndon shouted at Dennis "right, now stop it now, stop it, I am not putting up with this stop it Dennis, come here." Lyndon wrapped his arms around Dennis and comforted him and he calmed down but went totally silent and just sat there and mum and Lyndon cuddled him and she calmed down and said "oh my god, I knew this was going to happen a few weeks ago, I just knew it, he knew it also I could tell by his ways and now it has come true, are you allright den?" Dennis was just sitting there totally numb and never answered his mum, Lyndon stopped crying and said I had better phone Mel and Danny immediately. Lyndon picked up the phone and dialled and Danny answered and Lyndon said "hi Dan it's Lyndon I am afraid I have got bad news dad died a few minutes ago on the slab while having his operation and before you say anything, he lost about a cup of blood so it was not that he was just too weak to carry on." Danny said "is mum allright and Dennis?" Lyndon "not really and Dennis is the worst I am a little worried about him." Lyndon puts the phone down and said "Danny is on his way home, I will call Mel" Lyndon called Mel and Mel answered and said "oh dear, flipping heck I knew as soon as you answered the phone to me he was dead, I felt it, well he has passed on to be with Christ and god in heaven now they just as well throw his old body on the compost heap now." Lyndon snapped "oh yes I really need to hear that don't I? Here talk to your mother" he handed the phone to mum and went outside for a fag. Mum was crying and Mel was as cool as a cucumber saying "don't cry mum he is going to see you again in paradise soon enough it's just his old body that's left and I will be up later and we can get everything sorted out ok? I am leaving soon as I have had a bath see you soon, stop crying mum its allright." Mum puts the phone down and goes and sits by Dennis who is sobbing his heart out and they cuddle and mum says "I know den he was a pain in the ass but we still love him and he wants us to get on with living and be happy I am sure so let's dry our eyes and smile and think about the times we all had together especially the good old days out on the motorbike and sidecar." Den started crying even worse than ever as soon as mum said that and it seemed as if den was inconsolable.

Later that night they were all there Mum, Mel, Dennis, Lyndon and Danny all looking as if the world had come to an end and yes Dennis was still crying and it was a worry for the rest of the family to see him like this Mel says "c'mon den we must smile when we think of dad, he would not want you to keep on crying, I know it's not fair but we need to keep it happy for him and mum,." Den nods and gets up and goes up the stairs and mum says "he is taking this hard I am worried about him he thinks dad will be coming home and no one can convince him any different." Danny chirps up "well he will have to get used to it mum or it will cause him a lot of problems." Mum "remember he is mentally handicapped and we don't know how his mind and heart is taking it all probably much more severe than us so let's be gentle with him ok? I mean it." They all nod in agreeance and den stayed in his room all night and never came down and mum popped in to see him and he was standing looking out the window down towards the coast watching the lighthouse flashing in Porthcawl and he said to mum as she came in "look at the lighthouse flashing I wonder if dad can see it from Cardiff, I bet he can and we will miss him and I want to buy him some pansies for his funeral as he always grew pansies and them funny face flowers in the garden." Mum smiles and says "yes, that's a good idea and the funny ones were call funny faced viola's we can pick some from the garden in the spring and put them on his grave is it?" Dennis scratches his head nervously and says "I don't want to see his grave after the funeral I have got him in a photo and in my head all the time, how are we going to manage without him mum? He was always here and now never any more, what will we do with his things and his car?" Mum smiles back and says "we will keep a few things to remember him by and the rest will go to charity as that is what dad would want us to do and the car is old and not in very good condition so it will be scrapped, I expect as Lyndon says it will cost too much to get it fit for to sell." Den with a tear appearing in his eyes says "ok I will help and Mel will take the books and things of dads and I will keep the books about the war ok and can I have his watch he had in his pocket? And the tape machine on his desk." Mum nods and says "I don't see why not, he would be happy as long as you look after them ok? A huge smile appeared on den's face and he wiped his eyes and says "yes I will look after them no problem; I am going down stairs to see Mel."

Downstairs it was thick in the air with sadness and Danny and Lyndon were about to go down the club for a few pints and Dennis says to Mel "so where is Abby and the boys, I thought they would come down with you." Mel says "OH they are staying with their mother and they were very upset when they heard about their grandad so I thought they would be better off with their mum but you will see them in the funeral Den and they are looking forward to seeing you." Den brushes his fringe over to one side then said "is Abby big now I haven't seen her for ages it will be nice to see them again, I am having dad's watch and his cassette player mum said I could." Mel looking surprised said to mum "I was hoping to have his watch mum den can't even tell the time and I am the oldest." Mum did not know what to say and then said "sorry Melvyn but Dennis asked me and it's not worth much and I said he could have it so get used to it I don't want any troubles here now he has gone I had enough trouble when he was alive so leave it at that "den says "I am mentally backward and I will learn to tell the time ok." Mel said "allright sorry den you have it and I will find something else to remember him by, I know I will have his book collection if I can mum what do you think?" Mum smiles and says "oh yes please that is ok I will be glad to see the back of them he never read one of them so take them." Danny and Lyndon started to laugh and Mel asked them what their were talking about and Danny replied "we don't want any of dad's torture implements such as his slipper his belt and any of the stuff in his shed ha, ha, ha." Mel solemn faced says "I don't think you are funny it's your dad you are talking about." Danny in a huff says "oh c'mon Mel let's not beat about the bush he was not a nice man sometimes was he? he used to beat the hell out of me and you know it he was a bully in his early days so don't make him out to be an Angel, I have struggled to cry since he died and it's because he was such a hard minded old sod and you went down to Milford haven to get out of his grip." Mel looked dumbfounded and says "no I didn't I went under my own steam, yes he ruled us with a rod of iron but he was not that bad, so don't say things like that." Mum got her ten penneth worth in and says "are you blind Melvyn he was a nightmare especially when he became a Jehovah's Witness so don't say anything else, he was not a nice man in the early days so let's leave it at that." Mel did not answer and Danny and Lyndon went off to have a couple of pints and Dennis sat there talking to Mel until the early hours of the morning.

It was the day of the funeral and it was a crematorium funeral and all done by the Jehovah's witnesses that did not go down well with Mum, Danny and Lyndon and there was no wake that was so strange and Dennis was broken hearted with it all and from that day on he was a changed man, he seemed to grow up over night and was such a caring man and a delight to know so gentle and mild and loved by so many people from that time on, a real gentleman but he always seemed to have a troubled mind. He would often look on at what other people did and how they enjoyed themselves and wondered why he could not do these things such as a close dance with a female have a girlfriend and one day a wife and why not many women went anywhere near him and this made him sad, a totally boring life just looking out of his bedroom window with his music playing most of the day. The world was enjoying life and he was not getting involved in anything, living in a remote village on top of a mountain and nothing going on from day to day and Dennis was stuck in this rut as Danny and Lyndon could just go out of the village and find entertainment but Dennis nothing just a void, nothing was happening for him. Dennis became a lost soul and his nature changed as he got to be a silent person not saying much and a lovely peaceful man who did not get involved with much and became a bit of a recluse a very boring life and mum was getting more worried about him and she had lost the will to go on much in her day to day ways and became house bound and fragile, her health was deteriorating fast, the war was taking it's toll on her and her hair was now turning yellow and she had severe trouble with her intestines and most of her body was not working as it should and she was very tired all of the time and it was obvious that the sulphur she put into bombs in the war was eating her away from the inside out and it was so upsetting for all her boys and Dennis helped her as much as he could and never backed down from helping her but Dennis and mum became stuck in the house at all times and this was not good.

Lyndon was now the man of the house and it seemed unfair that a man so young should be put in this position and became a carer for them both. Danny and Mel were both married with children and it was all left up to

Lyndon, even he could not get on with a normal life because he was relied on too much until he got taken up with drinking heavy sometimes with his brother Danny but he still looked after his mum and Dennis. And in 1990 she had been in hospital seriously ill and the lads knew she was not going to make it and she died in agony in the hospital and this was not good for Dennis he totally lost it and it was a terrible thing to see he was devastated and the boys did not know how he was going to manage his mind due to his mental disorder.

It was the night mum died and Lyndon had to tell Dennis "Den come and sit down we want to talk to you, I am sorry den but mum died today in the hospital, sorry mate." Dennis just broke down and cried his eyes out and that got the other boys crying again and Dennis bit his hand and shouted out "your lying she is not dead, she is not dead she is coming home to let me look after her I will call the police on you if you say that again , please mum come home, I need you here with me and Lyndon please come home please, Mel go and get in your car I will come with you,, and I will beat the doctors up if they stop me getting her home, c'mon, c'mon lets go." Mel now crying said "C'mon den she is gone and you must be good or mum will have been upset seeing you like this, please stop it now, let's remember mum as she used to sit in that armchair smiling and making faces remember? She would not want you to carry on like this she loved you and all of us and she would be crying now if she was here and want you to look after her house now ok?" Mel put his arms around Dennis and they all cried for a long time and after a while they sat there remembering many times of fun, they all had with mum and there was many times to smile about but somethings Adolf Hitler won many years after he was dead.

Mums funeral was attended by a huge amount of people showing how much she was respected and loved and it was a lovely send off for her and Dennis did not take it well he was in tears most of that day and in his mind just wanted to die but it shows how resilient he was he pulled his socks up and got on with his life as it was not much to write home about and she was also buried by the Jehovah's witnesses that did not go down well with Danny and Lyndon as she was mostly opposed to them and it made a mockery of her last days with dad as he made her life sometimes a misery. Even Dennis rebelled a little about this and a few days later Danny organised a service in her church in Pencoed where she was brought up and it was nice to see Dennis smiling again when he got to see his aunties, uncles and his cousins especially his uncle Gino and Marlene and Mable and Tony, uncle Mel and Marjory, alma and Leighton and his lovely cousins who all made a fuss of him and that day was a little special.

Now it was back to living like a recluse in Bettws and Lyndon had a wife at last who took over mums position in the household b but she turned out to be a gold digger and an evil woman who would make Dennis's life even more boring etc.

Chapter 8

The family down fall.

Mel's life changed as he was now married with 3 lovely children, Danny's life was the same with a family and 5 children, Lyndon's life was now very different he had a new daughter and was now married and Dennis, well no change there at all his life went along as it always was he was just getting older and more sad by the day and then a change was about to happen Lyndon's wife decided to move from the family home as she did not like it there and drag Lyndon and Dennis along with her plans whether they wanted to or not. Dennis however was so excited about all of this and had no idea how this was going to turn out. It was all arranged and they left 51 Heol Glannant after living there for over 40 years ever since the house was built in 1954 a bit of a trauma for Dennis and maybe Lyndon, well they arrived in their new old house in Bettws off the beaten track of the main road for all the busses and it was a cul-de-sac no through traffic, not what they were used to, and the first week was fine for Dennis and then he realised it was not for the good, he realised he could not see the busses going pass the house and could not wave to the drivers he got used to seeing every day of his life and this was very upsetting for him and of course all his neighbours were gone no one to say hello to every morning like the Mullin family the Owens, Kendall's, Martinsons, and many more this was not what he thought it was going to be like and this made him more introvert and non-existent and this showed but Lyndon and his new wife just got on with their lives without a thought and of course Danny and Mel did not think of all of this as it was just something they should have realised would happen with Dennis but it was all left up to Lyndon.

Dennis however absolutely loved his new niece Eleanor to pieces and played with her all the time just like a doting father would ,and that's all he had to look forward to every day from then on and things between Lyndon and his new wife were very strange, she was only interested in what she could get out of life and Lyndon, she was always with her mother who was a hypochondriac and a real pain in Lyndon's life always demanding things and Lyndon did it no question and Dennis was virtually left to his own devices and of course Lyndon and his wife were getting good money from the government for Dennis and she would find a way to spend it on herself and Eleanor and Dennis was always in clothes that were shabby and he looked a mess, sometimes the same clothes for a year and Lyndon and his wife spent the rest on booze as Lyndon was well on the way to becoming an alcoholic by now due to all the pressure he had gone through looking after mum and Dennis which Danny and Mel felt awful about but did nothing to help.

Dennis ate anything he could get his hands on and it was always convenient food like pasty and chips from the chip shop packets of digestive biscuits, chocolates and all the rubbish that is not that good for you and he became a diabetic and this would change his life and yes it was all left up to Lyndon to sort this out but he had so much going on in his life this was the last thing he needed and his wife did not give a damn about anything except herself Eleanor and her mother and of course the social club in Bettws she would never miss along with Lyndon.

Dennis life was going downhill fast, he lost a lot of weight and he had to have insulin injected into him twice a day and he was not capable of doing this himself and so Lyndon had to do it or Dennis would die and it was another serious problem for den as it showed, it was the first week and it was not easy to get Dennis to take the insulin especially with Lyndon on the drink with no patience at all with it all and we felt it was too much for Lyndon in the end. Dennis was waiting on the armchair sweating and worried and Lyndon came in with his needle and said to Dennis "right den take your jumper off and roll up your sleeve." Den face went white by now and he done as Lyndon said and said to him "you are careful now I am sore on my arm and be careful ok?" Lyndon said in reply "just do as I say and let's get it done den out of the bloody way, I am not happy having to do this either so stand still." Den put his thumb in his mouth and looked the other way not to see it and he jumped as Lyndon such the needle in and Dennis said "oh bloody hell Lyn that stung you know do it slow." Lyndon "well keep still then it will not hurt I don't like doing this either mate but it has got to be done so get used to it, it's all left up to me all of the time." Dennis in a bad mood pulled his sleeve down and put his jumper on in a real mood then said "I hate it when you give me a needle and the nurse in the hospital never hurts me, you're a bully sometimes." Lyndon smiles and says "right den, ok I am going to get attitude from you every time I give you your injection, go and have a wash and no more digestive biscuits please, you know you are not to have any the doctor told you didn't he so leave them alone." Dennis stormed off to his room for the day and you could tell by his expression he was a very unhappy man.

Dens life had hit rock bottom and this showed he looked so helpless all skin and bone and it reminded me of a butterfly so flimsy gaunt and lifeless like a butterfly being pushed around while flying in the wind and the shape of Dennis's head reminded me of a butterfly a sorryful sight to see with the beauty of a butterfly but at the beck and call of anyone who wanted to use or abuse him. Den often turned to tears he was so bored and his life became non-existent and he began to lose the will to carry on and his brother Danny could see this and decided to talk to his older brother Mel they got together in Milford Haven when Danny was working down there and the meeting went just like this.

The 2 brothers met and sat down to talk and Mel asked Danny "so what is the problem with Dennis then?" Danny trying to be tactful said "his health is going downhill badly Mel this diabetes is bad, Lyndon is drinking like it is going out of fashion, his wife don't give a damn about Dennis he is dressed like a vagrant his clothes are dirty all of the time and I don't think he gets any money, they both spend it on drink in Bettws club nearly every night and on babysitters for Eleanor, I think it is too much for Lyndon and he looked after mum with great difficulty and now Dennis. He has not had a life that is normal and a bad start to his marriage so we need to do something now immediately." Mel pondered and looked sad then replied "so what do you suggest Dan I am too far away to help." Dan "I know Mel but I think we should think of putting Dennis in a home for people like him to give him some sort of life, he is just sitting in his room deteriating and that is not good and Lyndon and his wife could do with the break, what do you think? Mel looked shocked and replied "that's a bit drastic Dan isn't it? Things are not that bad, I don't think that is necessary, do you?" Danny says "yes I do it is not working is it and Dennis needs a new life or at least a life as at the moment he has got nothing and it is breaking my heart Mel it needs to be sorted." Mel could see the logic of what Danny was saying and nodded in agreement and then replied "so where do you suggest we put him, I will help as much as I can let's sit on it for a day or 2 and then speak again, get our heads working on a resolution for this, what do you think" Danny smiles and agrees and says "he will qualify with the money he receives from the government as I have checked and there is no problem, the only thing is Lyndon and his wife will lose his money and it will cause a real stink I think with those 2." Mel looked amazed and says "do you think so?" "Oh yes she will have to get a job to carry on the way they spend money on beer and they will not like it" Mel "oh dear so how will we tell them?" Danny says "no worries I will tell them and it's tough Denis comes first and that's that "Mel looked shocked by all of this but went along with what Danny said and they decided to meet up again a week later.

Danny went back home and decided to confront Lynden with this while he was on his own and he asked him to come over Danny's house to talk.

Lyndon walked in and sat down with a serious face and Danny commenced "how are things with Dennis over there? he looks really down lately don't you think? I was wondering how you felt about him going into a home for people like him?" Lyndon pondered on this for a moment and replied "why? What are you trying to say? I am not looking after him well enough for you?" Danny hurriedly said "no, no, no, that's not what I am saying I just thought it would be a good idea for him to be with people like him and give you and Denise a break as you have not had a single day together alone since you met her and I know Dennis will be happy there, I have spoken to Mel and we both agree it's time for you to have a life for you Denise and Eleanor." Lyndon looked shocked by this all and said "looks as if you have made your minds up already." "oh, don't be like this Lyn it's not like that at all we are thinking of everyone in this matter not just Dennis." Lyndon sat back and thought a little then said "so where are you thinking of putting him?" Danny "no idea really we are just tossing it around in our minds until something is decided one way or the other" Lyndon then said "don't you think you should ask Dennis about all of this? "Danny replied "that is my next question, would you mind if I ask Dennis over this Sunday for dinner and speak to him about this, you can come over too if you like. "Lyndon did not know what to say at first then said "no you go ahead and do what you like Dan I will not be here mind but I will tell him. "Danny looked nervous and said "let's not make this an issue Lyn I am thinking about Dennis in all of this he has not got much of a life and he is in his mid-40's time to do something for him to enjoy and if he insists, he wants to stay with you then ok no problem, agree? "Lyndon agrees and off he went to see Dennis and this he did and phoned Danny to say he will be over for his Sunday dinner and Danny smiles hoping for a nice result.

Well Sunday came around and Dennis showed up early to see what Danny wanted to tell him and Danny greeted him and Dennis was rubbing his hands together excited and he did not know why and he said to Danny "Allright Dan and Sheila it's nice out there with the sun shining isn't it? "Sheila said to him "Yes, it is Den and I have not finished the dinner yet so sit down and you and Danny have got a cup of tea each so sit down and enjoy it, I must get on" Danny and Dennis sit down and Danny said to him "right Den how would you like to move down by Mel and start a new life down Milford way near Mel. "Den looked shocked and serious and puzzled and said in serious voice "what do you mean? Live with Mel and Morrice you mean, I don't mind, what about Eleanor I want to see her mind. "Danny said "oh I don't know about living with Mel I thought in a big home with people like you and make friends even look for a girlfriend, what do you think?" Dennis looked shell shocked and worried "I am not going to Hensol castle no way forget it I want to go home. "Danny tried to calm Dennis down "No not Hensol Castle it's a house like this one and people share the house no nurses or doctors honestly and you will have a room to yourself and your own telly and radio and you will have friends to talk to and lots of girls there, isn't that nice? No one is going to do anything to you I promise and I will be coming to see you regular and Mel and Lyndon and the rest of the family and you can come home when you like to visit. "Dennis sat there not saying anything and puzzled over what Danny said then smiled and said "So there will be girls there like me? What about their fathers they will shout at me if I go near them?" Danny "no they won't they will not be there, remember when you went to the centre in Aberkenfig it is like that but you will live there, I mean the people there will be like those people but instead of seeing them now and again you will all be living in a big house together having breakfast together, dinner together and having fun and going out in the minibus and having holidays together." Dennis by now was smiling from ear to ear and he looked as if he had won the lottery, his face said it all, he then said" That sounds nice, so I will look after myself, will I?" Danny explains "well there will be someone to cook for you and a few carers to look after you all and help you with anything you need and take you out shopping and I will come to see you there and bring you up here to see Elanor and have dinner here and spend a day or two as a visit what do you think?" Dennis liked the sound of this and said "When will this happen then? I need time to get ready and pack all of my things you know." Danny stopped den "Steady now Den I have got to talk to Mel and Marice yet to arrange everything and Mel is calling me tomorrow night to work it all out." Dennis started brushing his fringe to one side that he always does when excited and said "I will tell Lyndon and Elanor and Denise too and I am looking forward to going to Milford haven, how long have I got to get ready?" Danny looked serious and said "It should not take long I don't think I will let you know as soon as we have decided on a place and see what you think." Dennis replies "I am excited about this and can see Burt and the girls in the Kingdom Hall I haven't seen them for a long time now and Gerald and Shirley and John Barnett and his wife."

Next thing Sheila called them as dinner was ready and Dennis could not stop talking all about this and kept on and on for days that drove Danny, Sheila, Lyndon and Denise nuts.

Mel finally called Danny one night and surprised him on how he wanted to do this. "Hi Dan, how are you? I have had a word with Morrice and we would like to have Dennis to come and live with us, what do you think?" There was a bit of silence from Danny and then he said "Are you sure Mel? I am surprised he might be the same there you know doing nothing all day and you are in a remote area in Milford." Mel replied "Well we can give it a try and see how it goes and I am sure he will be looked after well here, I am worried about sending him into a home as mum and dad fought all their lives to keep him in the family with us all so let's try it and then go from there." "Ok Mel I agree and when do you want to do this?" Nel stuttered a little and said "what about 2 weeks Saturday? I need to get the room sorted out and get Lyndon to sort out his stuff I don't want a load of crap sent down lets get this started in a way we all are happy about; can you help by sorting his clothes out? And don't send televisions or radios down except his little transistor, I have got everything like that here it's like curry's here in this house ha, ha, and it's a chance for Den to wreck some of them so as I can chuck them out ha, ha, ha." Danny laughing on the end of the phone said "Yes he is good at that, I will sort things out for him and I am sure Lyndon will help. Are you coming down to pick him up or shall I drive him down for you?" Mel "No I will pick him up as Morrice and Abby want to go shopping in Cardiff." "well Mel will you give him a ring and tell him he will be so excited he will be packed by the morning and I just had a thought Morrice will be better at giving him his diabetic needle as she is also a diabetic so that will work out fine, lets hope it works out for the better. Mel" I hope so Dan if not it will be plan B and I will look for a home near me as it is lovely living around here and he will love it in the end, right Dan I will call him now, speak in the week"

Mel called him immediately but spoke to Lyndon first "Hi Lyn I am ringing to speak to Dennis but I am going to run this past you first, I want Dennis to come and live with us as I feel it's about time you had the help needed to have a proper married life and we can look after him and if it does not work out we will go for plan B what do you think?" Lyndon was not crazy with the idea but agreed with Mel then said "So when is this going to happen and what do you want me to do with his stuff?" Mel replies "2 weeks Saturday I will come down to pick him up and just pack the best of his clothes and no tv's or large radios I have got plenty to go around and we will take him shopping for some new clothes ok? And try to explain to him he has got to get rid of some of his rubbish he is like dad keep anything he finds I have not got much room in his bedroom as it is. "Lyndon says "yes ok Mel I will sort him out and do you want to speak to him now?" "Yes, please let's see how he feels about it all, speak soon Lyn." Dennis is called from upstairs and speaks to Mel "Hi Mel you allright I am busy today sorting out all my cards with the busses and lorries out so what's the matter?" Mel then said to him "How would you like to come and live with me and Morrice and the kids?" Den's face lit up and he said hurriedly "Yes ok, but where will I sleep?" Mel "you will have a bedroom to yourself and a telly and radio is already here so do not bring them with you as there is no room, we will take you shopping for new clothes ok?" Dennis now very excited rubs his hands together and then brushes his fringe several times to one side said "Yes I will and are you picking me up tomorrow then?" "No, I need to do your new bedroom yet and so it will be 2 weeks on Saturday to give you time to sort all your stuff and get rid of your rubbish ok?" Den still smiling from ear to ear says "I will be ready and tell Abby and the boys I am going to help them with anything they want to do. "Mel replies "Yes ok I will tell them and you must help Marice when you get here and keep things tidy here for me and the boys are looking forward to you coming here and so is Abby, speak soon allright?" Dennis smiling says goodbye to Mel and was so excited he went up to Denise and Lyndon and says "I am off to live with Mel and Mar now and I will be popping home to see you and Eleanor and I will be having my own room down there, that's good isn't it?" Lyndon says "yes Den and you will have to sort out all the stuff you have got and get rid of some of it ok? Mel has not got the room for any of your rubbish so start sorting it all out tomorrow and things will be easier and Danny will be picking you up from time to time to come and see us all and I think you will be happy with Mel and the weather is much better down there not much snow mind." Den "oh dear, I like the snow so I will come home in the winter to see it and make a snowman with Eleanor and I will miss Smokey and Bandit and they will miss me I expect." Lyndon says "aren't you going to miss me and Denise then?" Dennis with huge smile says "yes I will miss you and little Josh but I will like it down there I hope and I will see all the witnesses in the kingdom hall like John Barnett and Gerald and his wife Shirley and we will be going down by the sea side sometimes ha, ha, ha." Lyndon "you are making me jealous Den I will be still mending cars and will have to make my own tea now, never mind as long as you are happy aye?" Dennis went off to his room to start sorting things out and Denise says to Lyndon "it will be strange without Den here won't it? And Eleanor will miss him and are you allright about all of this?" Lyndon replies "what choice do I have they have all decided and I have not got much to say about it all I just hope Danny and Mel know what they are doing, so let's leave it there ok?" Denise agrees and walks off.

Well it was time for Dennis's move with Mel and Dennis stood by the gate all morning waiting for him to turn up and then Danny turned up in his car to see him off and he said to Den "Allright mate?" Dennis all excited rubbing his hands together and a massive smile on his face replies "He is late I think and so you will come down on the weekends to pick me up, then will you?" Danny smiles and snaps "oh no I will not, not every weekend just now and again matey." Dens face went serious and he does not look happy and says "Why not?" Danny "no way, I am not coming down there every weekend maybe once a month it's a long way den but you will be allright you will start a new life down there ok?" Den looks nervous and says "what about Eleanor I want to see her Dan." Danny "sorry Den but it is impossible for me to fetch you every week and Eleanor will be in school most of the time but I will pick you up at least once a month, don't worry and you must start getting on with your life Den maybe find a girlfriend and get a small job down there and you will be off for holidays in their with the people around you with similar things like you have." Dennis looked very worried and said "I don't think so but I will try and find a girlfriend do you think there are girls down there then?" Danny smiled and said "oh yes of course there are girls down there more than there are here in Bettws it's lots bigger than here and maybe you can find something to do down there, Mel will sort you out don't worry" Next thing Dennis got jittery as Mel pulls up to pick him up and Dennis run to the driver's door and opened it and said excitedly to Mel "Aha your here Mel at last, Lyndon is in the house and do you want a cup of tea before we go?" Mel replies "oh hello Den let me get out of my car first and give me a hug mate." They hugged and then Mel said "now that's better and yes I will have a cuppa before we go and a biscuit if he has got some ha, ha, ha, hello Dan everything allright?" Dan replies "I think so I haven't been in the house yet as Den was standing by the gate when I pulled up all excited about his move but nervous I think but he will be ok soon as you pull off, it's a big move for him all he has ever known is Bettws and his bedroom so we will have to pay a little attention for a while to him until he settles down." Mel "yes I am also a little nervous about all of this but it will be fine I am sure and if it does not work out, I have got a homme in Neyland if needs, and it's Burt Rees daughter works there Denise and she says it is lovely there so there is a contingency plan set up but I am sure it will work out." Danny smiles and says "Oh brilliant Mel as I feel he will not be settled with you as it is a little remote and he gets anxious if he is on his own too much and I think he will be too much for you and Mar as he can be a handful, but we will see." Mel "Well I hope he will settle he is in his 40's now he is getting old now and if he does not, I can arrange things with Denise and her boss Colin pretty quick and I will not be far away for him and you have got a lot of work down there you can visit him as much as you can that will be good for him." Danny says "Yes I have already told him this and he is happy but thinks I will be doing this every weekend but I just can't " Mel smiles and replies "well it might be a good idea to bring him home at least once every 3 weeks to start with and then let it die out and maybe one of us can bring him here once a month until one day he will be happy enough to not want to come down here so often it will work out don't worry." Next thing Dennis came out with a huge box and put it in Mel's car and then 2 cases and a bag and they were about to leave and Lyndon, Danny and the other 2 boys said goodbye and Dennis all smiles says "right Lyndon look after Elanor and everyone else and I will see you next week and I will probably be having lots of fun down in Mel's place but will talk to you on the phone so, so- long see you keep smiling ha, ha, ha." They all laugh at Dennis and how he said goodbye and they pull off and they are gone and Lyndon says to Danny "well there he goes a new chapter in the Duckfield household I will miss him not being around, in fact it already feels strange with out him it's going to be weird here now, I just hope he will be happy now." Danny looked sad and says "I know Lyn it will be strange as it does already but he needs a life now he is always looking lost when I see him it will be good for him and I hope we will be saying this time next year look at him now a new man and having a fantastic life at last." Lyndon looking down to the ground says "I hope you are right, time will tell" Danny got into his car and left and Lyndon went to his outside wall and leaned on it and looked very sad by all of this.

CHAPTER 9

Life begins at forty plus.

Dennis first day down with Mel and family went off fantastic he had a continues smile on his face and loved being there with Seth, Jarrad and Abby but they were all in work or school in the day and so he got bored and Morrice was not a well lady herself and suffered with type 1 diabetes and could not pay Dennis all the attention he needed as being Mentally handicapped he can be a handful and in time this proved his down fall there and so Mel called Danny and Lyndon to explain that he was not settling down there and he said " hi guys It is not any good with Dennis here as he is often left alone with Marice and is sometimes too much for to handle him so I have spoke to Denice and she has spoken to her boss and there is a room there for him so I have arranged for him to go there, it is a lovely place with around ten people there and all like him and he will love it there, I am taking him down there tomorrow to see what he thinks about it so what do you think?" Danny says "well I am all for it I think he will be happier with people like himself and he will settle down immediately, what about you Lyn?" Lyndon replies "well I don't know what to think I wonder what is going on in Dennis's head about all of this but I will go along with this as long as if he is not happy, he has the choice to come home here ok?" Both brothers agree and things are set up for the next day.

Mel speaks to Dennis after the call and says "Right Den I am taking you to Neyland house tomorrow to see if you like it there and you know Denise Burt's daughter she works there and will help you settle in there if you like it there ok? And there are lots of people who live there like you and I think you will love it there, what do you think?" Dennis scratches his head nervously and replies "Where is it? And what about seeing Eleanor and who will be there I know? I know Denise she is nice, what about my stuff? And my records and telly? I need them mind, is it safe for me there?" Mel stops him and says "Calm down Den I will be back and fore to see you every day until you settle down and Danny will be in to see you regular and you will have your own room take all your stuff there and you will have your own room and key to it and make lots of good friends there and go out on outings in their mini bus and I will give them my telephone number so you can call me anytime and I will come down and take you out sometimes ok?" Dennis looked much calmer and said "Oh I see, all right but what if I don't like it there?" Mel says "I will come and take you home to Bettws then." Den looked unsure but smiled and went into deep thought. He didn't sleep at all that night wondering how things are going to turn out for him.

Monday morning and Mel and Dennis on the way to Neyland to see where den was going to live and Dennis looked as if his world had come to an end, he enjoyed the lovely views of the haven and stunning waterways and he then seen for the first time his new home and his eyes lit up, a stunning large house with palm trees in the gardens some benches to sit on and it was overlooking the haven and Dennis eyes lit up when he seen a lady he knew, Denise Burts daughter and a few people sitting on the benches talking some of the inmates of Neyland House. They pulled up and met with Denise and she introduced Dennis to the others "Dennis this is Ken, George and Lilly, they all live here in the house and you will be spending a lot of time together and I will take you in to meet the boss." They entered the building and met immediately the manager of the home Colin and he immediately said "Hello Dennis, welcome, it's nice to meet you at last I am Colin and if there is anything you need, I am here to help you any time ok? Hello Mel, I have got a nice room for you Den and a radio clock by the bedside and Denise will be looking after you for the first few weeks is that ok?" Dennis overwhelmed by this had a huge smile on his face and said "Oh right ok is there a telly in my room? And have I got a key?" Colin with a massive smile said "Yes you have got a key and for food you must come down to the lounge and it will be served to you at all times and I know you have a few injections for your diabetes and this will be done by your carers no problem and this week we are going out in the minibus for a picnic on the beach down the coast, do you fancy that?" Den smiling even more by now says "Yes ok, ha, ha, ha, any beer with it?" Colin "oh you like beer, do you? Maybe a few Shandi's, fancy that? Mel speaks "How shall I do this Colin should I come back for a few days until he settles in?" Colin "Maybe Wednesday and see from then on but I think he will settle immediately, what do you think Den?" Den "I'll be all right it's nice here and I will help with the bus I had buses in Bettws, I love busses." Colin says to Denise "will you take Dennis around and show him the home and the house he will be in down the road and then we will meet for a cup of tea in the lounge in fifteen minutes." Dennis and Denise went off and Dennis looked as if he had a new toy and Mel said to Colin" I hope he is going to be all right." Colin says "Of course he will be all right it's a new adventure and he will see the benefits immediately you will see." Mel says in concerned voice "You will call me if it goes, wrong, won't you?" Colin smiles and says "Of course I will Mel but he will be all right believe me."

Later they met up with Dennis and Denise for a cup of tea and Mel asks Dennis "So what do you think den? It's nice here isn't it?" Dennis all excited replies "I have got a huge room down the road and there is a play room with a snooker table in it and the lads were playing on it and said to me they would teach me to play it, ha, ha, ha, and I want to be over there later to listen to music in the lounge and there's girls here too, ha, ha, ha, and they are going shopping on Saturday and I am going with them but I have not got any money." Colin says smiling "Don't worry Den I will give you your pocket money every Thursday and you can spend it on something in Milford on Saturday and you will be getting pocket money every week ok?" Dennis face lit up and he said "Oh right, can I buy a record with it?" Mel says "it's your pocket money den do with it what you like as long as there is no sweets or biscuits ok?" Den agrees and asks to go off to his room and off he went looking so happy,

He got to his house and met up with a lad and hit it off with him immediately he was a man with similar problems as Den and he asked him his name and he said "My name is Kenny and I am a fast runner you know, who are you?" Den says "Oh I am Dennis and I am a bus driver but I had to leave them back in Bettws I was not allowed to bring them down here, nowhere to park and I love lorries and fire engines, do you like them?" Kenny looks puzzled at Dennis and replies "No I don't I have a brother who takes me out on his boat sometimes and I have got to wear a special jacket so I will not drown in the sea and he is coming to see me later I will ask him to let you come if you like." Den looking worried and scratching his head snaps "No it's all right I am afraid of the water and my mum told me to stay away from water but I like snow and last year I was hit by snow balls and threw some at the lads in our street, why is that bell ringing?" Kenny smiles and says "it's time for coffee and tea, in the lounge coming?" The lads go off for drinks and in there were all the other inmates in that particular house and Dennis was introduced to them all and got on with them like a house on fire. This was a relief for his brothers who were basically left out of Den's life for a few weeks as he was so happy there.

Well a few months went by and Dennis was so happy and Mel popped in from time to time and Dennis was always so busy with his new friends he had little time for Mel and so life was good at last for him and one day he was called in to see Colin and he said to Dennis "Hello Dennis, how are you? Do you like it here?" Dennis answered "Oh yes it's nice here and I got a nice room and some new friends, why?" Colin says "Oh just asking Den, I have got a problem and I was wondering if you can help me, I need a volunteer to go and stack some shelves in theCo-op up the road, do you fancy trying it and they will give you money for working there a few hours a week." Den scratches his ear and looked puzzled and said "Oh I don't know I have never done anything like this ever what if I get it wrong? Oh, I don't know." Colin smiles at Den and says "it will not matter they will help you get it right and they have asked for you so I think it will be good a working man it will be safe so fancy giving it a go? I will come with you for the first few times ok?" Dennis still looking worried says "And you will show me what to do all right?" Colin reassures him and Dennis face lit up with a huge crooked smile and he ran off to tell Kenny and his mates.

Well Dennis got his job in the co-operative and enjoyed it for several months and soon got fed up with it and he gave it up but was amazed that in Neyland the younger people there did not make fun at all at him, this was a boost for him and he lapped it up and went out roaming the town more and more and getting more confident by the day. Sometimes he got a little upset not seeing Eleanor, Lyndon and Bettws but it was a new life and over time he got used to it. Dennis was very clever he used to have his dinner in this house up the road from Neyland House where he lived and then he would go to the big house and say "well I have not had food yet and am getting hungry and they would feed him for the second time, so was he that stupid? I don't think so. Danny picked him up many times and took him to Bettws for the weekend and this helped and soon after he was moved into Neyland House the main home and there were more inmates there and he soon got his feet under the table however he was not doing well with his diabetes and this showed and from time to time his room was searched and lots of packets of digestive biscuits were discovered and this was not good for his diabetes and there was no changing him he would not stop buying and hiding them once he made his mind up there was no changing it he was very stubborn on everyone and in time this would cause him lots of grief.

It was one day he started talking to a woman there her name was Janet and she was a lovely lady and so innocent in her ways and Dennis and Janet got on very well and Dennis one day got very serious with her he said "So are you Married to anyone then?" Janet giggling replied "don't be silly, I can't get married I have had no one to marry and my mum said I will never marry anyone because I am ill in the head." Dennis said "So am I, but I like you a lot can we be friends you know." Janet "oh I don't know Dennis what do we do as friends then?" Dennis smiling from ear to ear and scratching his ear says "we can hold hands sometimes like they do and you can lean on me on the couch when we watch telly." Janet looking uncertain says "We are not allowed, are we? I will have a row." Dennis "no we won't we are old enough now and if I want to hold your hand I will and tell them off if they shout at us ok and you can be my girlfriend if you like." Janet went all silly at this and could not answer him at first then said" Do you think it is all right? I might get sent to bed early mind." Dennis" Aw no they won't send you to bed we are old now so they will watch us I expect mind but I can be your boyfriend if you like." Janet now turning her head in embarrassment says "Oh dear I don't know, I like you and must be good and you must ok? I am having a biscuit, do you want one of my biscuits?" Den looks excited and says "Oh yes please, I will be told off if they see me eating biscuits because I am diabetic ha, ha, ha, so don't tell anyone ok?" Janet smiles and replies "Will you die if you eat too many biscuits?" Den "No don't be silly it just makes me tired but one will not hurt, shall we go and sit in the garden on the seat out there? It's nice out there, the sun is shining and I need to get a tan." Janet nods yes and off they go and out on the bench was Kenny and David and Den said to them "Hey c'mon move over for me and my girlfriend to sit down in the sun." Kenny says "That's not your girlfriend that's Janet by you." Den "Yes, she is my girlfriend aren't you Janet? Go on tell them." Janet looked confused and stood up and ran off indoors and Dennis looked upset and shouted to her Hey Janet where are you off to?" but Janet carried on walking straight up to her room and never looked back, this upset Dennis badly and he could not understand why she ran off. Kenny says to Den "See she is not your girlfriend she has ran off to cry in her room ha, ha, ha, ha." Dennis went into serious mood and snapped at Kenny" Don't be an idiot she is my girlfriend but she is shy I think and stop laughing or I will hit you and tell the carers you are making fun of us." Dennis got up and went inside to see if he could see Janet but she was gone and Den sat in a large armchair looking as if his birthday had been and gone.

It was the next day that Janet reappeared and Den did not know what to do she did not speak to Dennis and averted his gaze and Den was wondering why and what he has done and that is how it was all that day and for a few days after. It was one evening and Dennis walked into the television room and seen Janet watching telly and he sat down and just watched telly not saying a word and then in Walked one of the carers and said to them "Hi guys what's happening?" Dennis and Janet just shook their heads and said nothing and the carer started to laugh and said "Aren't you 2 speaking to each other I was told that you are boyfriend and girlfriend is that right?" Still they said nothing just looked at the carer and the carer then said "Right what's the matter? I am not leaving this room until we have sorted this out so Dennis tell me what's wrong, c'mon tell me." Dennis lost for words said "I like Janet and want to be her boyfriend but she thinks we will get into trouble if we do, so tell her." Carer asks Janet "So what is wrong with you Janet tell me." Janet starts crying and says "I don't want to get into trouble and I will be told off if we hold hands or sit by each other and I am afraid." Carer smiles holds Janet's hand and says to her gently as den looks on sadly. "Who said you would be in trouble Jan?" Janet "Everybody, my mum, my dad, and my friends and Kenny." Carer replies "Well you will not be in trouble and if anyone says anything to you tell them to go away as it's ok as long as you are both sensible, I can see by Dennis's face he likes you very much and I think you like him, do you?" Janet says "I don't know if it is all right, I don't want to get into trouble." Carer smiles holds Janet's hand and says "Janet it is all right you are a grown up now and it's all right to have a boyfriend and sod the rest of the people here and what they think it's none of their business so stop getting yourselves upset and have some fun and no one will say anything ok?" Janet smiles at hearing this and Dennis's face changes to happiness. Next thing the carer carries on with her work and Dennis gets up and sits by Janet and there was a long pause as if time stood still and then Dennis grabs Janet's hand and you could see the love between them and they held hands like 2 birds with a broken wing it looked so strange and they sat together for around 2 hours in the same position and cuddled until midnight and they had huge smiles and it was love at first sight between them both. Next thing a carer walked in and Dennis and Janet jumped and let each others hand go still worrying that they might get into trouble and the carer then said "Oh hello, it's the love birds, do you know it's nearly midnight and time for bed, we are all so happy to see you 2 together and in love it's so lovely and I have warned Kenny not to stir the shit or else so C'mon give each other a kiss and see each other in the morning I will be back soon as I have taken the cups into the kitchen ok?" off the carer went to give them time to say goodnight and it was so funny as they all of a sudden kissed and it looked so awkward as they were in their forties and never knew how to kiss but it was so loving and off, they went to their separate beds with a huge smile on their faces. Is this going to be good or bad for these 2 loving people or will someone spoil it for them as they felt so unnerved by all that was happening and wondered if it will last or will someone put a stop to it, time will tell.

Well it was one weekend later and Danny was about to call in to take Dennis home to Bettws to visit his family there and Danny walked in to wait for Dennis and Dennis was sitting drinking tea and Janet was washing up a load of dishes and Den got up and shook Danny's hand and was so excited he said "all right Dan I am having my cup of tea and then we can go, do you know who this lady is? This is Janet she is my girlfriend you know." Danny looking a little stunned by this said "Oh hello Janet nice to meet you, I didn't know you had a girlfriend Den you sly old dog you." Janet looked straight ahead and ignored Danny probably because she was shy and Dennis acting like a child with a new toy says "oh yes, she is my new girlfriend and we are having lots of fun since we met and she loves me and I love her don't we Jan?" Janet said nothing still being shy and Danny chose his words carefully and says "oh that's nice for both of you I am so happy for you both and is Janet living here also?" Janet mumbled "Yes I am on the same floor as Dennis and we enjoy being together don't we Den?" Dennis smiling from ear to ear says "oh yes, we are good with each other and we are in love you know." Danny "I am so happy for you both, right den lets go and I am parked outside ok lets be off, nice meeting you Janet see you soon, bye." She says bye and Dennis says "I am ready and lets go then." Dennis while passing Janet pats her on the bum and says "Ta, ta, see you tomorrow Jan be good mind." And off the lads went for Bettws.

In the car and all that Dennis kept on about was Janet, it was obvious he was very much in love with her, is this possible and everyone in the past was wrong about Dennis state of mind and he really had feelings like this almost as normal as everyone else? Danny was puzzled by how Dennis was whilst talking about this lovely lady he really was in love with her. Danny's mind was now working overtime as he has never seen Dennis in this new light it felt normal and right and Danny was not about to burst his bubble and began to think it is possible that Dennis was acting normal and that he had met his partner in life and they would love each other for the rest of their lives and why not. Dennis was like a nutcase he talked so much about Janet and Danny just sat there listening to it all wondering where this was going from here as Dennis and Janet were almost living together well all but, Danny needed to talk this out with his brothers but Lyndon was being awkward towards Danny since Dennis left his home to live in Milford Haven and so Danny kept a low profile and Dennis was staying the first night with Lyndon and family.

They arrived in Bettws at Lyndon's house and Dennis immediately kept on to them about his lovely lady Janet and Lyndon was very curious about her and asked Danny "Who is this Janet he is keeping on about Dan?" Danny replies "She does exist she is real, I met her in the Neyland house they both live at and she is lovely she really is and he is besotted with her he even slapped her on the backside as we were leaving it's the real thing I think." Lyndon looking serious says "don't be silly he can't have a serious girlfriend he is mentally retarded, nothing can come of it can it?" Danny "well I don't know why not? He is very much in love it seems to me, why not? I would not like to burst his bubble." Lyndon "are you serious? I don't know what to think I never thought of Dennis getting a woman in his life, I suppose it's possible, oh I don't know I am confused." Danny "well Lyn he shows lots of regard for her and he is so happy I never thought he would ever find anyone and I am shocked but it's nice to see that lovely crooked smile he has got on his face isn't it? I don't think anyone can get in his way with this and I for one will back him up all the way in what ever he decides, what about you? I think he has had enough of a traumatic life since he was born fighting everyone and everything time for him to have a life now and he is so much in love, look at him for goodness sake I have never seen him so happy." Lyndon shook his head and said with a smile "yes your right, he looks so happy and alive, doesn't he? I am with you." Dennis kept on about Janet all that night and the next day when he went over Danny's for dinner. Sheila dan's wife says to Dennis "so you have got a girlfriend now then Dennis?" Den puts on a lovely loving smile and replies scratching his ear "oh yes she is in the same home as me her name is Janet and she likes me a lot and we hold hands sometimes and lean on each other in the TV room and sometimes we kiss each other you know and we go out walking as well she is my girl you know." Sheila says "that's nice Den and is she welsh or what?" den shrugs his shoulders and says "oh I don't know but she is nice and I will bring her up here soon to meet you all ok?" Sheila "that would be nice and I may call in with Danny in the summer to see you all, that would be nice wouldn't it? And we can go and have a meal in Neyland somewhere ok?" Den smiling all over says "ok I will tell her and she will be excited to see you all, you will like her she is nice." Well after dinner Dennis was starting to hint to go home to see Janet, he kept on about coming home to see Lyndon Eleanor and Danny Sheela and Josh and soon as he gets here, he goes on about going home to see Janet and Danny realised, he had lost Dennis to Janet and Pembrokeshire and he was totally in love.

Danny realised this was for real and as soon as he got Dennis back to Neyland house he was in such a rush to get into the building to see her and Danny got out and tried to keep up with him but it was impossible so Danny went in and sat in the lounge and Dennis came back in and said "she is not here, she has gone shopping with Denise, oh well like a cup of tea or what?"" Danny replied "I would love a cuppa thanks Den." Den goes off to make one and someone speaks to Danny one of the carers there she said to him "oh hello, your Dennis brother, aren't you?" Danny "Yes I am he has gone to make me a cuppa and he has had a good time home in Bridgend with us all but could not wait to get back." Lady says "o to see Janet I expect they are connected at the hip most of the time but she has gone to do some shopping with Denise." Danny smiles and says "Yes I know and Dennis was not too pleased he run in here to find her and his face when he realised, she was not about was a picture ha, ha, ha." Lady "I can imagine, they are very much in love and you cannot separate them on times but it's lovely to see." Danny looking down to the floor says "Yes, I know, I think we have lost him as a family and I didn't think this would ever happen, so what do you think about it? Honestly now." Lady looked a little shocked by the question and says "I think it's nice for them both why should they not have a lovely life after all they are getting on in age now and I will back them up in whatever they do it almost brings tears to my eyes sometimes when I see how happy they are." Danny thought for a minute and says with a huge smile on his face "Yes you are right its fantastic and I am also so happy for them both I agree." Next thing in walks Janet and Denise and Dennis hears her forgets about Danny's tea and rushes to see Janet he says to her "Hello, where have you been was looking for you, I am back ha, ha, ha." Janet in a loving sounding voice says "oh hello Dennis, how are you? I missed you did you have a nice time when you went away? I have bought you some sugar free chocolate." Dennis smiles totally forgets about Danny and his tea and off he goes with Janet and Denise says I will finish off the tea Dan his head is somewhere else." Danny "Thanks Denise I have never seen him like this before I am stumped, I will drink this and be off I will not get any sense out of him now ha, ha, ha."

Danny left Dennis in his lovely home with his lovely lady and smiled for a long time thinking about Dennis and Janet and how much in love they are and decided to call on Mel just about 2 miles from Neyland and he got there and Mel greeted him as usual with a hug and smile another brother with a heart like a lion and they went inside his house and sat down for a cup of tea and Danny said to Mel and Morrice "I just left Dennis and Janet in Neyland house and am amazed how much in love they are with each other I am so happy for them it's nice to see him so happy Mel." Morrice replies" I know I seen them a week ago and he is a different man these days and always with Janet, they are never apart according to Colin, he's a lad, isn't he?" Mel says "he makes me laugh he always finds me on a Tuesday night when I go to the book meeting in Neyland he is there as soon as we arrive there right on time every time and he wants to talk forever ha, ha, but he never misses getting there to bug me ha, ha, ha." Danny smiles and says "I know he is not as stupid as everyone makes him out to be and he is obsessed with Janet." Mel "well he is certainly happy there now and set up for life there now I think I have never seen him so happy." Danny smiles and says I think this is the real thing Mel we have lost him and I am so happy for him in love at last and the engagement next." There was a deadly silence and Mel looked awkward and then said "what do you mean? It's just a friendship I think." Danny "do you think so, I don't I think he is in love totally and why not let him have a loving relationship just like anyone else in this world, surely you can see he is in love just like anyone else just because he is retarded it has not affected his feelings and Janet was so pleased to see him when he got back it was heart wrenching I almost had a tear in my eyes Mel you should have seen them so much in love, honestly." Mel "yes but nothing can really come of it can it his mind is not capable of living like a married man, "Danny "why not Mel? Why not?

Are you going to tell him this it would break his heart and I for one am for it never mind which way you look at it he is in love and to try and put a stop to it would probably kill him and Janet so I am not going to stop his future he deserves a fantastic life with her after what he has gone through in his short life, don't you think?" Mell put his head in his hands and thought for a while and then smiled and said "Yes I suppose so, I never really thought about until you just said what you did." Morrice says "well he is not a stupid man, is he? He definitely knows the difference between love and hate so why not let it go and see in a few weeks how it turns out then get together and discuss it again." The both lads thought for a minute and then Danny said "well I am for it and I don't think things will change by what I seen there today and this weekend for that matter , but then there is Lyndon Mel, he is drinking even worse now and is becoming a Alcoholic mate for definite , things are not good I am trying to slow him down but he is on destruction mode at all times and that bloody wife of his is a waste of time no help at all." Mel looking sad says "oh no, is he? I was hoping he would be over all that I am worried now but what can we do?" Dan says "not a lot Mel if he does not want to listen then it's hopeless, there is no talking to him he denies anything is wrong we will have to just wait and see what happens and I will keep on his case to try and get him to stop." Mel "One brother gets his life sorted and another one steps into hell, and I hope you are ok, I know you drink a lot too." Danny "yes but I can take it or leave it I have got a job that makes it impossible to drink like he does I love a pint but I can say no also so don't put me in his category Mele am no saint but not stupid either." Mel "right Dan I must get ready to go to a meeting, take your time driving home and keep me up to date with Lyndon ok and we will talk again in a few weeks about Dennis and Janet ok?" Danny gets up and leaves and thinks about Dennis and Janet all the way home with a wry smile on his face.

Dennis and Janet love for each other got stronger and stronger and this showed to everyone they were in contact with and never a cross word between them ever like an old married couple and Dennis was approaching fifty now and I had no idea how old Janet was but they looked good with each other so much so in the end no one expected anything else between them.

It was a few weeks later that Dennis was called into see Colin and asked if he wanted to do some more work outside the home, Colin says "well Dennis how do you fancy doing some work for a few days a week for some pocket money?" Dennis answers "oh I don't know I will not see Janet so much and she will be sad." Colin smiles and says "yes Den but you need to earn some money for any holidays we all go on you know and then you will be able to get things for Janet as well, she will love that." Dennis "we can save up to get married mind and get a nice wedding cake, ah yes that will be a good idea." Colin was taken back in what Dennis said and stammered and said "oh I don't know about that, why do you want to get married Den?" Dennis scratches his ear and says "I don't know, we might as well we like each other and we have been together now for ages and Janet says it's ok, and Danny and Mel will be happy, won't they?" Colin sits there for a minute and ponders and says "well Dennis I was not expecting that for one minute are you serious about getting married?" Dennis with huge smile and excited says "yes, me and Janet said this a few days ago and she will be nice in a wedding dress and was excited when I said it and hugged me a lot that night and we can get married here in the home." Colin "well we will have to see Den I must talk to your brothers first see what they think and we will talk about it again ok? And Janet's family will need to be talked too, leave it to me Den I will talk to them all first." Den got serious and says "it's nothing to do with them., none of their business is it just me and Janet." Colin tries to cool Dennis down and says "of course it is Den but they will want to know, won't they? Lets talk about it in a few days and in the mean time I will look out for a small job for you ok?" Den nods yes and walks out of his office to find Janet.

Den finds Janet and said to her "hello there, I am getting a job to save for our wedding ha, ha, ha, Danny and Mel will be shocked ha, ha, and we can be Mr and Mrs. if I get a job that is, we must have a big wedding cake and some friends to say nice things about us and then we will have to live in the same room together." Janet's face said it all she was so excited she nearly fainted and said to Den with a loving look "oh that would be nice Dennis and I will wear a wedding dress, I have never had a wedding dress before or nice flowers in my hand to throw at the end of the day, are you excited Den?" Den with huge smile on his face and almost a tear in his eye replies "oh of course I am and we can sleep together then and there will be no need to get up so early to find each other and we can watch telly late at night and have a cutch, and I will make you tea in bed and keep you nice and warm ha, ha, ha." Janet still excited says "oh yes we can it will be nice won't it Den?" Den "I will have to get a job as soon as I can now, and you will have to learn to make cakes and cook now mind." Janet's face dropped with worry and she said "oh Dennis I can't cook and they told me it is too dangerous for me to do this, sorry, we will have to buy cakes from the shop and eat in the dining room here unless you learn to cook Den." Den scratches his ear and said "I can make tea and sandwiches and that's all but never mind as long as we get married aye."

Well Dennis went with Colin for an interview in a local garage and den looked very serious about all of this and the owner of the garage says to him "hello Dennis pleased to meet you, do you like nice shiny cars?" Den replied with a smile on his face "yes and busses and lorries." Man said "do you fancy cleaning my cars inside and out and make them nice and shiny?" Dennis scratching his ear looked ill then said "no your all right thank you " he then proceeded to walk to the door and waited for Colin to go and Colin says to the garage boss "oh right, I am sorry but it's his decision and when Den makes his mind up there is no changing it but thanks for going to the trouble I really appreciate it, goodbye" Colin shakes his hand and looked embarrassed and left the garage but never asked Dennis why he did not fancy that job den was stubborn that way. Back in Danny's house a few days later a phone call from Mel and Danny answers it and Mel says "Hi Dan, are you sitting down?" Danny ponders and says" why what's wrong? Dennis is all right, isn't he?" Mel "oh don't panic it's nothing like that but Colin has spoken to me and says that Dennis and Janet want to get married." There was a deadly silence and Mel then said "Hello are you still there?" Danny then said "yes I am just surprised and didn't know what to say but I had a feeling this would happen after speaking to him the last time he was up here, well what do we do?" Mel "ha, ha, ha, nothing can be done he will never be able to live like a family with Janet can he? How can it be done? we will have to just let it pass and say no more about it he will forget it soon enough." Danny goes silent for a minute and then says "Why not he and Janet are in love that is not fake is it? And if they can feel love what's to stop them living a fantastic life together, why not? Why not?" Mel says "are you serious? They are both mentally backward and we don't want them having any children that would be tragic for them and what will people say?" there was another deadly silence and then Danny says "who gives a damn what people say they have been on his back since he was born and probably the same for Janet and look how much in love they both are and they don't think or give a damn what anyone else thinks in their little bubble I don't think we really matter to them let alone anyone else, Mel they love each other and you have got to be blind if you can't see that I say leave them get married and be happy for the rest of their lives I for one will bless them when they do." A few minutes went by then Mel chuckling says "Dan you have got a point there and yes, why not? And as regards the baby situation we can discuss it with them to use some sort of birth control, I agree dan we must talk to them both as soon as we can yes why not." Danny says "Good Mel it's party time but we must not rush them into it but organise it all for them in a sensible manner and we will get it right just for them and our lovely brother Dennis who could do with a bit of luck in his life and let anyone say anything to me and look out he deserves to be happy and I have never seen that boy so happy since he moved down there and met Janet she is so good for him and I am now very excited for them both and since mum and dad are not around I bet they would be so happy for him well at least I know that mum would be so lets sort it out soon Mel." Mel then says "let's get it right in our heads first before we say anything ok?" Danny "I agree Mel I feel so happy for the both of them speak soon Mel bye" they both hang up and Danny started to cry and Sheila says to him "What's the matter Dan are you, all right?" Danny smiles and says "nothing things are fantastic." Dennis and Janet were very much in love and just like normal people it was true love you only had to look at them and it was so clear well Dennis got offered a job car valeting and Janet was so proud of her man and Dennis was so proud of her and at last life had started for Dennis no more bullying, no more people talking about him as if he was not there or as if he did not matter, no more poking fun at him and threatening him, no one now can hurt him he is in heaven as far as he is concerned Dennis and Janet were in a little bubble of their own and no one else matters to them they are so much in love even after 3 years together and Danny especially was excited to see him wed to his only love it was definitely a lives happy together for the rest of their lives just what they both deserve with everyone's blessing.

Life ticked on gently for the next few months and lots of talk with Mel Danny and Lyndon and it was decided to leave the winter months go by and wait for the nice weather to arrive before arranging their wedding and the lads never said much to Dennis but waited until the bad weather had gone this was going to be something the boys were looking forward to and still worrying a little also how this would be taken with family and relatives but it was going to happen.

It was mid-winter and it was breakfast in the home and Dennis was always dropping off to sleep every morning without fail and the others were all fussing over breakfast and Janet had not got up yet so den dozed off on the couch and then one of the carers asked him what he was having for breakfast and he did not answer and she asked him again "Dennis c'mon I have nearly finished everyone's breakfast except yours what would you like?" there was still no answer from him and so she shook him and said "hello Dennis I am talking to you wake up Den " but he never moved at all she tried again then shook him hard and he still never moved and the carer panicked and sent everyone out of the room and called for help and another woman came in and they both tried to wake him shouting" Dennis wake up, Dennis wake up oh my god he is not responding get him on the floor quickly and give him cpr " they got him on the floor and pumped his chest while the other carer called 999 and it was in no time the response team arrived and continued to pump his heart and just then Janet was heading for the dining room and they got to her before she walked into the room and diverted her away in time. The first response team said to the carers "oh I am sorry but he has had a massive heart attack there's nothing we can do he is dead I am afraid "everyone started crying and straight away someone took Janet out for the day before anyone had time to tell her

Everyone was crying in the home that morning and they called Mel and just closed the door and locked it to the dining room until Mel arrived.

In the meantime Janet was out in town with a carer and saying "why am I having breakfast in town I wanted to be with Dennis for breakfast as we were going to sit in the garden in the sun and talk about the wedding and eat some biscuits with tea" the carer says "oh sorry Janet but it is so busy in the home this morning I thought you would like to have breakfast with me in town I needed the company." Janet says "oh ok, I can see Dennis a little later and I can get him some nice cakes he likes is that ok? Carer almost crying could not answer for a minute then said "yes of course., but we will go to Milford haven first and you can get them there." Janet agrees and off they went.

Back at Neyland house Mel arrived and was in total shock and went in to see where Dennis was and they unlocked the door let him in and Colin said to Mel "I am sorry Mel there was nothing anyone could do it was a massive heart attack and he was only 54 so young we will miss him so much and Janet has been taken out for the day and she has not been told, I don't know how I am going to tell her it will ,kill her, here we are oh my god look at him such a lovely man taken so young, Mel I will leave you alone with him and come and see me before you go." Mel says "yes of course Colin see you later." Mel walked up by the side of Dennis who was still lying on the floor and a tear appeared in mels eyes and he bent down and kneeled to the side of Dennis and his eyes were still wide open and Mel put his hand over them and closed them and said "oh Den I am so sorry, you were such a lovely man and we will miss you." and Mel then said a prayer over him and then Mel burst into tears and just sat with him until the coroners officer turned up and put him in a coffin and took him away. Mel went into Collins office and there was a tear on Collins cheek also and they talked about Dennis for a while then Mel was off to let the rest of the family know, he phoned Danny first and it was by now early evening and Danny answered the phone and Mel said "Hi Dan I am afraid I have got some bad news for you, Dennis died this morning of a massive heart attack." Danny just screamed out loud "no, oh no, no, no, oh no it can't be he is too young to die please tell me your lying it is a dream no, no." Sheila Danny's wife jumped up and said" what is the matter? What is it?" Danny with tears rolling down his face says "it's Dennis he died this morning." Sheila just put her hand over her mouth and said "oh my god, not Dennis he can't be dead he was such a lovely man and him and Janet oh my goodness how sad, I am so sorry." Mel on the other end of the phone said "Dan are you all right I am worried about you now as you are not that well either "Danny still sobbing uncontrollably says" it's not happening he was about to get married to Janet and live happy ever after just like he planned it oh Mel why?? Why? Why? Why him he had a fairy tale ending left to live out with Janet oh no, and how is Janet?" Mel says "They took her out for the day before she would find out and so they are keeping it from her somehow." Danny oh that poor girl she will not be able to take the loss of Dennis this will, kill her if she finds out." Mel "tell me about it I don't know what Colin will say to her and I am about to let Lyndon know he will be besides himself and I will call you tomorrow about the funeral arrangements of I am not able to talk much longer it has upset us all down here speak tomorrow and look after yourself." They ring off and Danny just burst into tears.

Danny said to Sheila "oh my god, it's not fair just as he had sorted his life out and was so happy he drops dead, if there is a god he has got an awful sense of humour, I need a whisky to toast such a lovely man we have lost then I will phone all the relatives, why him? Why?"

Back in Neyland house and Janet had arrived back and was straight away off to look for Dennis and she could not find him anywhere and went to see Colin and said "I can't find Dennis I have got some cakes for him you see and I can't find him, do you know where he is Colin?" Colin trying hard to hold the tears back said "Let's have a seat Janet I have something to tell you, Dennis has gone away for a while he is not well and he has got to go and get better and he will not be coming back for a long time." Janet looking puzzled says in concerned voice "no he hasn't he is all right I seen him last night where is he please Colin?" she starts to cry and not understanding what is happening looks so sadly at Colin and Colin says "Janet he has had to go to a hospital a long way away as he is ill, I promise you and he has asked us to look after you until he gets back so don't worry ok?" Janet just did not understand and got up to go and look again for him and they got a nurse to give her a small sedative to help her sleep as she was so upset and Colin just came back to his office and shed some more tears. It was going to be a while before Dennis gets cremated and Colin decided not to take her to the funeral and just to the wake in Milford after it as she will not realise, he has been cremated and just meet all the family there.

It was surprising the amount of people in his funeral it was jammed packed with relatives and friends from Milford and all over Pembrokeshire and many from his home village of Bettws it was like a convoy of cars going down the M4 to see that lovely man off. It was revealed that Dennis had a huge stash of digestive biscuits hidden so well in his room. On the day of his funeral it was so sad and his coffin was so light in weight as Dennis was like a butterfly so slim and fragile looking, the day went off fine first a speech in the Kingdom hall and then down to Narberth to get cremated and Mel Dennis's big brother took charge of the funeral at both venues this took a lot of guts and determination on his behalf and then it was off to the wake at the seafront in Milford Haven and the day was so lovely as regards the weather it was so sunny all day for him.

In the hall all were sitting down having some food and next thing Janet made her way around everyone and shook their hands and all of the time not realising Dennis was dead and this was his funeral wake she approached Danny, Mel, Lyndon and said to them as they listened "Dennis has gone away and he is not coming back where is he then? "this was so sad and it took a lot of nerve to not burst into tears and then Danny said "Janet he is ok he was asking about you and always does ask about you he is happy and he wants you to be happy ok? I know he loves you very much and misses you" Janet just nods and you could see she really knew Dennis was dead. Next thing she went on to meet others and Mel got up and walked out of the building across the road overlooking the beautiful haven of see and it was so sunny and Danny followed him out and said to him "Allright Mel I know how you feel just like me when Janet said those words I nearly cracked up and had to hold it just for her and Dennis." Mel bowed his head and said "I know I was the same I keep on thinking it is a joke and he will creep up behind me and make me jump, I wish he would dan I miss him he was such a gentleman." "I know Mel I keep on thinking he will turn up and say ha, ha, ha , caught you ha, ha, he was such a lad and often confused me with his ways and yes I will miss him so much he has always been there I can't imagine not having him around, but he is out of his misery now although he was so happy with Janet and he loved Neyland house and all in there and he loved Pembrokeshire I think we did the right thing bringing him down here don't you?" Mel wiping a tear off his cheek says "of course it was he had a whale of a time here and was so happy this I know for sure " Danny says smiling "well there we are then we did the right thing and I only wish he had the life he had here in the last 4 years in the first 50at the beginning of his life instead of all that crap he had to put up with bless you Dennis we will miss you." The lads put an arm around each other shoulders and went back to the wake.

It was a few weeks later that the close family had a get together in Pencoed cemetery near Bridgend where their mother was buried and they had his ashes put in the grave with his mum and even that brought tears all round that day but they were all happy he was back with his loving mother to look over him.

We all miss the loving brother son and man who brought so much love and happiness to this drab world and often wonder how it would have been with Dennis and Janet married and being so happy I feel they would be something proud to see and if the world had so much love and care for each other it would be a world worth living in. I certainly believe he has now settled on another planet somewhere out there and has been born again to a world that will see a lot of love from him and hopefully he is as normal as you and me, whatever that is.

Janet still lives to this very day in Neyland house and is in her 70's but now suffers with dimenture but is still a loving woman that Dennis loved to his dying day without Question and she made him so wanted and she loved him to bits.

Well that was Dennis's life for what it was worth even though he lived a tortured life he found love in the end and that was worth seeing his face so happy as he always was, now no one could hurt him ever again.

Well Denisse brothers life did not last much after him, Danny who is still alive and wrote this book lives in Pembrokeshire now but went totally blind a few months after Dennis died, his little brother Lyndon died of alcoholism 2 years later at the age of 42 and big brother Melvyn John died ten years later aged 63 of an aneurism. All the brothers died or went blind within ten years and it was Dennis who was the main key in that family as he kept them all on their toes for 54 years and Dens dad Raymond George also died of serious heart problems at the same age of 54. If there is life after death it's likely that Dennis came back somewhere as himself and if he did there will always be lots of love wherever he is, bless you Dennis wherever you are.

His only uncle left alive on his mums side that Dennis loved so very much as they often had a good laugh together was so kind to do a hand drawing of den of him for the front of this book that has made this such a loving tribute to Dennis and Janet and I would like to thank him for doing this out of love for Dennis and to those people who loved him as much as we all did so thank you Gwyn Stone.

The picture on the back of this book is of the lovely village of Bettws in the Garw valleys, a beautiful village we as brothers grew up in and I would like to thank the people of Bettws who showed a lot of care for Dennis and in his later years got to love him as we all did.

I would like to give a huge thanks to Neyland House and all the staff there who made Dennis's and Janet life complete and the love and the care for Den and all the times they made me and my brothers life going to see him so comfortable and easy, also the medical care they gave him to make his life so easy.

There are so many people these days with similar problems that Dennis had but these days they say they have learning difficulties and if only they realised this in those days his life would have been much better and to those who have got these learning difficulties look at the way Dennis lived his life and was not put off many times by doubters but embraced life and showed the world how to love as you are all so special to us all and a real delight to us all. So, keep on trucking and be noticed at all times because you are really so special.

Butterfly

By Dan Melynden

Just like a butterfly with lonely eyes, he was born in a world full of lies

Fighting against the wind from the moment until he dies

A funny little man with a loving crooked smile

His nose was bent with parts of him missing and some would run a mile

Born in a world of hate and fear

A fool on a hill and people made this clear

A body of a man a face of a clown

is he a freak or has god let him down?

He smiles with love and looks you in the eye

A loving man to simple to cry

He turned a key into another world

He would suffer hate that people would hurl

Just like a butterfly flying against the wind

Pulled and pushed around, in a previous world had he sinned

He just couldn't do wrong he just couldn't do right

But everything he did he would always have to fight

His love for you and his love for me was always so clear to see

His smile he showed was done with a beam so lovingly

So thin so gangly a butterfly he could have been

Struggling in the wind with a loving facial grin

Then one day he fell in love with another little butterfly

Just like himself they flew against the wind together

They found their selves together for life

No more worries or evil strife

They only knew how to love, they only knew how to care,

This was all they were born to do this loving pair

His life was fulfilled he wanted her as his wife

And everyone agreed this would be so very nice

They lived so happily from that day on

Until one day there was an awful storm

Love would be struck that horrid day

The storm got our butterfly and like a leaf, he blew away.

THE END.

Printed by Amazon Italia Logistica S.r.l.
Torrazza Piemonte (TO), Italy